Civilian Health Insurance Options of Military Retirees

Findings from a Pilot Survey

Louis T. Mariano, Sheila Nataraj Kirby, Christine Eibner, Scott Naftel

Prepared for the Office of the Secretary of Defense

RAND

NATIONAL DEFENSE RESEARCH INSTITUTE and RAND HEALTH

The research described in this report was prepared for the Office of the Secretary of Defense (OSD). The research was conducted jointly by the Center for Military Health Policy Research, a RAND Health program, and the Forces and Resources Policy Center, a RAND National Defense Research Institute (NDRI) program. NDRI is a federally funded research and development center supported by the OSD, the Joint Staff, the Unified Combatant Commands, the Department of the Navy, the Marine Corps, the defense agencies and the defense Intelligence Community under Contract W74V8H-06-C-0002.

Library of Congress Cataloging-in-Publication Data

Civilian health insurance options of military retirees : findings from a pilot survey / Louis T. Mariano ... [et al.].
    p. cm.
    Includes bibliographical references.
    ISBN 978-0-8330-4127-2 (pbk. : alk. paper)
    1. Retired military personnel—Insurance requirements—United States. 2. Veterans—Health and hygiene—United States. 3. Federal Employees Health Benefits Program (U.S.) 4. Insurance, Government employees' health—United States. I. Mariano, Louis T.

UB448.C58 2007
368.38'20086970973—dc22

                                                                      2007016785

The RAND Corporation is a nonprofit research organization providing objective analysis and effective solutions that address the challenges facing the public and private sectors around the world. RAND's publications do not necessarily reflect the opinions of its research clients and sponsors.

RAND® is a registered trademark.

Published 2007 by the RAND Corporation
1776 Main Street, P.O. Box 2138, Santa Monica, CA 90407-2138
1200 South Hayes Street, Arlington, VA 22202-5050
4570 Fifth Avenue, Suite 600, Pittsburgh, PA 15213-2665
RAND URL: http://www.rand.org/
To order RAND documents or to obtain additional information, contact
Distribution Services: Telephone: (310) 451-7002;
Fax: (310) 451-6915; Email: order@rand.org

Preface

Traditionally, the U.S. Department of Defense (DoD) has provided generous health benefits to active-duty and retired service personnel and their families. For example, there are no enrollment fees for active-duty service personnel or their families for health care coverage. DoD retirees are encouraged to enroll in TRICARE Prime, which has an annual enrollment fee of $230 for individual coverage and $460 for family coverage—fees that have remained fixed since the plan's inception in the mid-1990s. Retirees and their families also have access to TRICARE Standard/Extra, which requires no enrollment contribution but has less generous cost-sharing provisions than TRICARE Prime. In contrast, worker contributions to employer-provided family health insurance coverage in the civilian sector averaged $2,713 in 2005, an increase of 46 percent over 1996 premiums (Kaiser Family Foundation and Health Research and Educational Trust, 2005).

Many DoD retirees work in second careers and have access to non-DoD health insurance. Yet the growing gap between civilian health insurance premiums and TRICARE enrollment fees makes TRICARE an increasingly attractive option vis-à-vis civilian coverage. As a precursor to implementing policies designed to control escalating costs, DoD would like to gain a better understanding of how many beneficiaries have access to civilian-provided health insurance coverage, even if they are not currently enrolled in civilian plans. Further, DoD would like to get estimates of average health insurance premiums faced by retired beneficiaries with civilian plans and the reasons beneficiaries may (or may not) choose civilian plans over TRICARE.

To improve its understanding of these issues, DoD asked the RAND Corporation to conduct a pilot survey of retired beneficiaries under the age of 65. This monograph reports on the results of a pilot survey of retirees fielded in early 2006. Retirees were asked about their employment status, eligibility for and enrollment in civilian health insurance plans, reasons for enrolling or not enrolling in plans for which they were eligible, use of TRICARE for medical care and prescription coverage, and responsiveness to changes in the price of civilian health insurance. The results offer useful information on retirees' health care status, enrollment in civilian health care plans, use of TRICARE, and sensitivity to changes in the price of civilian plans. Such information, combined with other data, can be used to analyze the effects of TRICARE benefit design changes.

This research was sponsored by the Under Secretary of Defense for Personnel and Readiness and was conducted jointly by RAND Health's Center for Military Health Policy Research and the Forces and Resources Policy Center of the RAND National Defense Research Institute, a federally funded research and development center sponsored by the Office of the Secretary of Defense, the Joint Staff, the Unified Combatant Commands, the Department of the Navy, the Marine Corps, the defense agencies, and the defense Intelligence Community. Comments are welcome and may be addressed to the principal investigators, Louis T. Mariano, Lou_Mariano@rand.org, and Sheila Nataraj Kirby, Sheila_Kirby@rand.org.

For more information on RAND's Forces and Resources Policy Center, contact the Director, James Hosek. He can be reached by email at James_Hosek@rand.org; by phone at 310-393-0411, extension 7183; or by mail at RAND Corporation, 1776 Main Street, Santa Monica, California 90407-2138. Susan D. Hosek and Terri Tanielian are codirectors of the RAND Center for Military Health Policy Research. Susan D. Hosek may be reached by email at Susan_Hosek@rand.org; by phone at 310-393-0411, extension 7255; or by mail at RAND Corporation, 1776 Main Street, Santa Monica, California 90407-2138. Terri Tanielian may be reached by email at Terri_Tanielian@rand.org; by phone at 703-413-1100, extension 5265; or by mail at RAND Corporation, 1200 South Hayes Street, Arlington, Virginia 22202-5050. More information about RAND is available at www.rand.org.

Contents

Figures

Tables

Summary

Traditionally, DoD has provided health benefits to active-duty and retired service personnel and their families. After 20 years of service, active-duty personnel can retire and are immediately eligible to receive retiree health benefits for themselves, their spouses, and dependent children. DoD retirees are encouraged to enroll in TRICARE Prime, which has an annual enrollment fee of $230 for individual coverage and $460 for family coverage. Retirees and their families also have access to TRICARE Standard/Extra, which requires no enrollment contribution but has less generous cost-sharing provisions than TRICARE Prime.

Since service personnel can conceivably retire in their late 30s or early 40s, many of these individuals are working in second careers and have access to non-DoD health insurance. Yet the growing gap between civilian health insurance premiums (estimated to be $2,713 on average for family coverage in 2005) and TRICARE enrollment fees makes TRICARE an increasingly attractive option vis-à-vis civilian coverage. Recent evidence suggests that employees are declining employer-provided insurance in favor of alternative sources of health insurance coverage, such as TRICARE.

In an effort to better understand the extent to which military retirees have access to and are enrolled in civilian health insurance plans, DoD asked the RAND Corporation to conduct a pilot survey of retired beneficiaries under the age of 65. The goals of the 2005 Survey of Military Retirees included the following:

- Estimate the percentage of retirees who are eligible for civilian health insurance, either through their own or their spouse's employment or through a union or a professional association.
- Estimate the percentage of retirees enrolled in civilian health insurance plans.
- Explore reasons for *not* participating in civilian employer health insurance.
- Estimate the premium costs retirees pay to enroll in their civilian health plans.
- Estimate how changes in civilian premiums would affect participation in civilian employer-provided health plans.
- Estimate the use of TRICARE facilities and benefits by those with civilian health insurance.

The purpose of this report is descriptive rather than analytical. We present a descriptive overview of the findings from the survey on the topics listed above. Follow-on work at RAND is using these survey results, combined with other data, to assess usage of TRICARE medical care and military facilities and the implications of benefit design changes on retiree behavior and health care expenditures.

Survey Methodology

The Defense Enrollment Eligibility Reporting System (DEERS) is a computerized database of military personnel and their families and others who are entitled under the law to TRICARE benefits. DEERS registration is required for TRICARE eligibility. We used the August 2005 DEERS to identify retired officers and enlisted personnel who were living in the continental United States (CONUS), were under age 65, and had been retired for at least one year (i.e., retired on or before June 30, 2004). We selected a stratified random sample of 1,600 military retirees, evenly split between officer and enlisted retirees, and administered a computer-assisted telephone survey that asked about the labor-force participation of the respondent and his or her spouse, eligibility and participation in civilian health insurance options, reasons for participation or nonparticipation, use of TRICARE and other coverage to pay for medical care, and the likely effect of premium increases or decreases on participation in civilian health insurance plans (if eligible). The fielding period was February–March 2006, with a response rate of 60 percent. Overall, 68 percent of the officers responded to the survey, compared with only 51 percent of the enlisted personnel. The sample observations were weighted, using probability of selection and post-stratification weighting, to account for the differential probability of selection produced by the sample's stratified design and to take into account the differential response rates among the strata.

Because the data reported here are estimates based on a sample, it is important to indicate the uncertainty surrounding the estimate. Here, we report the lower and upper bounds of a 95 percent confidence interval around the estimated population mean or proportion.

Findings

Employment Status and Eligibility for Civilian Health Insurance

Overall, 80 (77.1, 83.0) percent of the survey population was employed. About 78 (74.5, 81.8) percent of officers and 81 (76.9, 84.4) percent of enlisted personnel were employed. Eighty-seven (84.4, 90.2) percent of retirees ages 60 years or younger were employed, compared with 53 (43.6, 61.9) percent of those between 61 and 64 years. Most of the retired military personnel who worked were private-sector or government employees and most worked full time, especially those 60 years old or younger. Well over half—54 (50.0, 58.7) percent—of the retirees who were employed were working for large employers, with 500 or more employees.

Over four-fifths—85 (82.5, 88.1) percent—of the military retirees were currently married and living with their spouse. Fifty-four (49.7, 58.9) percent of spouses of officers and 62 (57.6, 67.4) percent of spouses of enlisted personnel were employed, and half (43.5, 53.9 percent) of these worked for large firms. Overall, 13 (10.7, 15.9) percent of retired military households had no one employed in the civilian labor force, 40 (36.3, 44.0) percent had one wage-earner (most often the military retiree in married households), and 47 (42.9, 50.2) percent had two wage earners.

Of the 80 (77.1, 83.0) percent of retirees who were employed, 82 (79.2, 85.7) percent were eligible to enroll in a plan offered by their current employer, and almost all of them (95.1, 98.7 percent) reported that their spouses and/or dependents were also eligible to enroll in such plans. Overall, of the survey population of military retirees, 65 (61.7, 68.7) percent were eligible for insurance provided by their employer and 58 (54.4, 61.7) percent of the population was eligible to enroll family members in such plans. Sixty-nine (64.6, 74.1) percent of retirees with employed spouses reported that their spouse's employer offered civilian health insurance and, of those, 89 (84.3, 93.1) percent reported that they and/or their dependents were eligible to enroll in the plan offered by the spouse's employer. The government and large private-sector firms were the most likely to offer insurance. Part-time workers had very limited access to insurance. Only 16 (12.8, 18.6) percent of the population reported being eligible for health insurance through another civilian source, such as a union or professional association.

If we count all sources of coverage for either the retiree or their families, we find that 78 (74.5, 80.9) percent of the survey population reported having access to some other form of health insurance for themselves and/or their families through their own or their spouse's employer or through a professional association (Table S.1).

Across the population, only 8 (5.4, 9.6) percent of military retirees were offered incentives by their own employer, and 3 (1.3, 3.9) percent were offered incentives by their spouse's employer, not to enroll in civilian insurance plans, but only 1 (0.2, 1.5) percent reported that such incentives were specific to TRICARE-eligible employees.

Table S.1
Percentage of Retired Officers and Enlisted Personnel Eligible to Enroll in a Civilian Plan and Those Currently Enrolled in Such a Plan, February–March 2006

Eligibility and Enrollment Status	Officers	Enlisted Personnel	Total Population
	Estimate 95% confidence interval (lower bound, upper bound)		
Retiree or family eligible to enroll in a civilian plan through an employer or professional association	72.9 (69.0, 76.8)	79.2 (75.2, 83.2)	77.7 (74.5, 80.9)
Retiree or family eligible to enroll but not currently enrolled in a civilian plan through an employer or professional association	35.5 (31.6, 39.5)	40.3 (35.4, 45.1)	39.1 (35.4, 42.9)
Retiree or family eligible to enroll and currently enrolled in a civilian plan through an employer or professional association	37.4 (33.1, 41.6)	38.9 (34.1, 43.7)	38.5 (34.7, 42.3)
Total percent enrolled in civilian plan (self and/or family) offered by employer, professional association, insurance company, and other	42.6 (38.2, 46.9)	42.1 (37.2, 47.0)	42.2 (38.3, 46.1)

NOTE: *Eligible to enroll* means that at least one family member (retiree, spouse, or dependent) was eligible. *Not currently enrolled* means that no family member was enrolled.

Enrollment of Military Retirees in Civilian Health Care Plans

Overall, 73 (69.0, 76.8) percent of retired officers and 79 (75.2, 83.2) percent of retired enlisted personnel were eligible to enroll themselves or their families in their own or their spouse's employer-provided plan, or in a plan offered by a professional association or union (Table S.1). However, half (45.9, 54.8 percent) of those who were eligible chose not to enroll either themselves or their families in civilian health insurance plans for which they were eligible. Overall, only 39 (34.7, 42.3) percent of the population was enrolled in an employer-provided civilian plan or through a professional association. Few retirees and their families were enrolled in health insurance from other sources—direct purchase from insurance companies or perhaps through Consolidated Omnibus Budget Reconciliation Act (COBRA) coverage. Adding enrollment through these sources, we find that 42 (38.3, 46.1) percent of the survey population was enrolled in a civilian plan and had either self- and/or family coverage.

Reasons for Enrolling or Not Enrolling in Civilian Plan for Which Retirees/Families Were Eligible

It is important to understand the reasons for enrollment in civilian plans as well as the reasons for not enrolling.

We first present reasons offered by respondents for enrolling in civilian plans. About half (48.5, 57.7 percent) of those currently enrolled mentioned that they preferred the network of doctors/hospitals in the civilian plan, while 49 (42.6, 54.4) percent reported the inconvenient location of medical treatment facilities (MTFs) as the reason for enrolling in the civilian plan. Thirty (24.5, 35.3) percent were eligible for free coverage through their employer or other non-TRICARE source. One-quarter (20.1, 30.2 percent) reported a lack of TRICARE coverage for needed medical care and the administrative burden and reimbursement delays associated with TRICARE as reasons for enrollment in civilian plan. Twenty (15.9, 25.5) percent said that their civilian coverage was less costly than TRICARE and, of this group, about half mentioned that the premiums were lower, as were the deductibles and copays.

Turning now to reasons for not enrolling in civilian plans, we found that the cost of the premiums was by far the most important reason for not enrolling in a civilian plan—mentioned by close to four-fifths (73.4, 82.9 percent) of those eligible but not enrolled, followed by high copays (58 [52.5, 64.0] percent) and high deductibles (57 [51.5, 63.3] percent). Half (45.0, 56.9 percent) reported that they preferred doctors in MTFs or TRICARE, and 30 (24.0, 34.7) percent said that the lack of choice with respect to doctors/hospitals was a factor in not enrolling. One-fifth (16.5, 26.5 percent) mentioned that the civilian plan did not cover care they thought they needed, while one-tenth (8.2, 15.7 percent) complained about the paperwork and reimbursement delays. A very small percentage of those eligible (5 [2.5, 7.6] percent) reported that their employer had provided an incentive to use the military coverage.

Premium Costs for Enrolling in Civilian Health Plans

According to a survey by the Kaiser Family Foundation and Health Research Educational Trust (KFF/HRET), in 2005, the average premium paid by an employee for employer-provided health insurance was $610 for single coverage and $2,713 for family coverage (Kaiser Family Foundation and Health Research Educational Trust, 2005). The KFF/HRET survey also reported that among covered employees in firms with three or more employees, 21 percent paid no premium contributions for health care coverage. In our survey, 21 (15.8, 27.0) percent of retired officers and 23 (16.5, 30.1) percent of enlisted retirees who were enrolled in civilian plans reported that they did not pay any premiums for the plans in which they were enrolled. About 16 (10.9, 21.7) percent of officers and 26 (19.1, 33.2) percent of enlisted personnel reported paying less than $1,000 per year for health insurance coverage, while 25 (19.0, 31.1) percent of officers and 23 (16.1, 29.8) percent of enlisted personnel paid $2,500 or more for health insurance.

As expected, annual premium costs varied by whether the respondent elected self-coverage only or family coverage. The average premium was $691 ($444, $939) for self-coverage only and $1,993 ($1,736, $2,249) for both self- and family coverage. The self-coverage figure is close to the $610 reported in the KFF/HRET survey for the same year. However, the average premium for family coverage was lower than that reported above in the KFF/HRET survey. This is not entirely surprising. These retirees have access to TRICARE coverage at very favorable rates, so they are unlikely to purchase other health insurance if it is expensive.

Price Elasticity of Demand for Civilian Employer-Provided Health Insurance

In our survey, we asked retirees who were enrolled in a civilian health plan what their response would be if their civilian premiums rose by 25 percent. About 42 (38.3, 46.1) percent of the survey population was enrolled in one or more civilian health insurance plans. Of these, about half (44.1, 58.5 percent) of those paying a premium reported that they would give up their civilian plan if the premiums rose by 25 percent. Thus, health plan enrollment, according to our estimate, is very elastic, –2.0 with respect to premiums, i.e., if civilian premiums increase by 10 percent, enrollment in civilian plans may decline by 20 percent. While this is a rough approximation, retirees appear to be quite conscious of premiums, and large premium increases for civilian health insurance may result in a substantial shift to TRICARE usage. Ringel et al. (2002) find that own price elasticities of demand for civilian health insurance range from –0.10 to –1.75, suggesting that enrollment is moderately to highly sensitive to premium price.

About 50 (45.9, 54.8) percent of the military retirees who were eligible for civilian health insurance had not enrolled in civilian plans. Asked whether they would enroll in these plans if premiums were to decline by 25 percent from their current level, very few—less than 10 (5.4, 13.7) percent of retired officers and 21 (15.3, 27.5) percent of retired enlisted personnel—reported that they would enroll in the civilian plan for which they were eligible if premiums fell by 25 percent, giving us a demand elasticity of –0.38 for officers, –0.86 for enlisted personnel, and –0.76 overall. Of the population as whole, only about 3 (1.8, 4.7) percent of officers and 9 (6.4, 12.0) percent of enlisted personnel would enroll in a plan if prices fell.

The sharp difference in the responses to questions about *increases* versus *decreases* in civilian plan premiums likely reflect a difference between those currently enrolled in civilian plans and those who have chosen not to enroll in those plans. Most retirees who are enrolled are paying a premium contribution, and their preference for civilian insurance does not appear to be strong enough to prevent their dropping the insurance if the premium *increases*. In contrast, retirees who have not enrolled in a civilian plan are probably avoiding a high premium contribution and would not reconsider their decision even if the premiums were to *decrease* substantially.

Use of TRICARE Facilities and Benefits

In 2005, 39 (34.0, 43.4) percent of all retired enlisted personnel and 45 (40.8, 49.7) percent of all retired officers received care at a civilian facility only, and another 12 (8.6, 14.9) percent and 16 (12.9, 19.0) percent, respectively, chose to go to a military facility only. Only 6 (3.8, 8.4) percent of all retired enlisted personnel and 2 (1.1, 3.5) percent of all retired officers received care at a VA or Uniformed Services Family Health Plan (USFHP) facility only. Some—between 15 and 18 percent—received care at two types of facilities, most commonly at a civilian facility and an MTF (11.0, 17.9 percent of enlisted personnel and 14.4, 21.3 percent of officers). We see a similar pattern among families of military retirees.

Retirees who were enrolled in a non-TRICARE civilian plan relied on a mix of both TRICARE and non-TRICARE civilian plans for medical treatment, despite being enrolled in civilian plans. For example, only 38 (32.2, 43.8) percent of this group said they relied exclusively on the non-TRICARE civilian plan, while 36 (30.1, 41.5) percent said they used both TRICARE and the non-TRICARE plan; 8 (4.8, 11.0) percent said they relied on TRICARE exclusively, with the probability of exclusive TRICARE use dropping significantly when the current premium costs for the non-TRICARE civilian plan were higher. Overall, 51 (44.8, 56.7) percent reported that they used TRICARE for all or some of their medical care.

Military retirees enrolled in a non-TRICARE civilian plan also relied heavily on TRICARE for coverage of prescription drugs. For example, while only 40 (33.8, 46.4) percent of officers and 30 (23.4, 37.3) percent of enlisted retirees enrolled in a civilian plan reported using only the non-TRICARE plan for prescription drugs, a much larger percentage relied on TRICARE (either exclusively or in conjunction with other coverage). Overall, 56 (50.4, 62.3) percent of retirees enrolled in a non-TRICARE civilian plan reported relying on TRICARE to some extent for their prescription drug coverage.

Policy Implications

DoD's fiscal year (FY) 2007 budget request proposed raising TRICARE enrollment fees, deductibles, and pharmacy copays for retirees to decrease the difference between cost sharing in TRICARE and civilian plans. Congress did not support these changes; the final authorization bill rules out any changes through the end of calendar year 2007. DoD hopes that narrowing the premium contribution gap would lead to a shift away from TRICARE, or would at least discourage further shifts to TRICARE. While price increases will undoubtedly lead to some decrease in the amount of medical care demanded, it is not clear how large the cost savings would be. The savings would depend on several factors—among other things, the relative rate of increase in civilian and TRICARE health insurance premiums and trends in accessibility to such plans in the civilian sector (given that some small firms are opting not to offer health insurance in the face of rising costs). In any case, as long as DoD premiums are considerably lower than civilian premiums, small increases in TRICARE premiums are unlikely to result in noticeable shifts away from TRICARE usage. Further, if TRICARE premiums remain stable while premiums in the civilian sector escalate, TRICARE usage is likely to increase.

Data from annual Kaiser Family Foundation and Health Research Educational Trust Survey (2005) indicate that civilian premium contributions for family insurance coverage increased by 46 percent between 1996 and 2005. Our findings show that while a substantial majority of the retiree population is eligible for civilian health insurance, about half of those eligible choose not to enroll, primarily for cost reasons. Our findings also highlight the fact that retirees (1) are extremely cost-conscious and might drop civilian coverage if costs of the civilian plan rose and (2) continue to rely on TRICARE for some of their medical care even if they enroll in a civilian plan.

The survey we fielded, while providing important information, was a pilot study with a small sample size. Understanding the potential impact of an increase in TRICARE premiums will require more complete information than we collected. For example, to fully model the impact of a premium increase for TRICARE, we need data on the civilian premium amounts faced by those who did not enroll, reasons for choosing to enroll in TRICARE Prime, and better precision on the estimates of interest than was possible with our limited sample size. Civilian employers may be considering multiple options for keeping their own expenditures for health care lower, including raising employee contribution amounts or entertaining the adoption of plans with higher employee deductibles and copayments. Since most respondents do not know the premium contributions, deductibles, and copayments required by health plans in which they are not enrolled, this information would need to be collected from employers rather than from individuals. In addition, the survey would need to ask directly about the impact of proposed changes in TRICARE fees and copays and about how likely future changes in civilian health plans are to affect use of both civilian and TRICARE medical care. A more complete understanding of choices and likely behavior in the face of increasing premiums and copays for TRICARE would require a larger survey that collected data from both retirees and their civilian employers.

Acknowledgments

The authors wish to thank several individuals for their guidance, insight, and support throughout this work. In particular, we are grateful to Wendy Funk for answering numerous questions about the data; Melissa Fraine, who patiently worked with us to get the data we needed; and our RAND colleagues Susan Hosek and Terri Tanielian for their leadership and advice in making this effort successful. We thank Robert Opsut, our TRICARE Management Activity (TMA) project officer, for reviewing the survey materials and for supporting our research efforts. We are grateful to Tim Elig and Anita Lancaster at the Defense Manpower Data Center, and to Denise Washington and Kim Frazier at TMA, who reviewed and approved the survey and helped us with the data use agreement. We thank Beverly Weidmer, Megan Zander-Cotugno, and their colleagues at RAND's survey research group for their contribution to developing and fielding the survey. RAND colleagues Melinda Beeuwkes Buntin, John Crown, Susan Marquis, and Jeanne Ringel reviewed our survey instrument and provided helpful comments, along with several anonymous RAND colleagues who responded to a pretest of the survey instrument. We thank them for their advice and participation. The report has benefited greatly from the careful and thoughtful reviews of Pinar Karaca-Mandic and Carole Roan Gresenz, our reviewers, who provided many helpful suggestions for improving the substance and clarity of the report.

Finally, we thank the retired DoD beneficiaries who took the time to respond to our questionnaire. Without their valuable responses, this effort would not have been possible.

Abbreviations

CATI	computer-assisted telephone interview
CBO	Congressional Budget Office
COBRA	Consolidated Omnibus Budget Reconciliation Act
CONUS	continental United States
DEERS	Defense Enrollment Eligibility Reporting System
DoD	U.S. Department of Defense
HMO	health maintenance organization
HRET	Health Research and Educational Trust
KFF	Kaiser Family Foundation
MTF	military treatment facility
PCM	primary care manager
POS	point of service
PPO	preferred provider organization
RVU	relative value units
SMR	Survey of Military Retirees
TMA	TRICARE Management Activity
TMOP	TRICARE mail-order pharmacy
TRICARE	nationwide health insurance plan for retired and active-duty military personnel, family members, and their dependents
USFHP	Uniformed Services Family Health Plan
VA	Veterans Administration

CHAPTER ONE

Introduction

Medical inflation, the expansion of benefits, and increased health insurance take-up rates among retirees have contributed to a near doubling of U.S. Department of Defense (DoD) health spending (from $14.6 billion to $27.2 billion) between 1988 and 2003. A recent Congressional Budget Office (CBO) analysis finds that if DoD's medical spending increases at the same rate as the per capita medical spending for the United States as a whole, total DoD health care costs could grow to as much as $52 billion by 2020 (in 2002 dollars) (Congressional Budget Office, 2003).

Traditionally, DoD has provided very generous health benefits to active-duty and retired service personnel and their families. Active-duty service personnel are required to enroll in TRICARE Prime, and their family members can enroll either in the Prime or the Standard/Extra plan. Regardless of the plan they choose, there are no enrollment fees for active-duty service personnel or their families. After 20 years of service, active-duty personnel can retire and are immediately eligible to receive retiree health benefits for themselves, their spouses, and their dependent children. DoD retirees who enroll in TRICARE Prime pay an annual enrollment fee of $230 for individual coverage and $460 for family coverage. Retirees and their families can also utilize TRICARE Standard/Extra, which requires no enrollment contribution but has less generous cost-sharing provisions than TRICARE Prime. A more detailed description of the differences between TRICARE Prime and TRICARE Standard/Extra is provided later in this chapter.

One of the probable reasons that DoD medical expenditures are rising is that *higher premiums for employer-provided health insurance coverage have increased retired beneficiaries' incentive to rely on DoD-sponsored health insurance (TRICARE), even when they have access to outside health insurance options.* For example, health insurance premiums for a family using TRICARE Prime—DoD's health maintenance organization (HMO) plan—have remained fixed at $460 since the plan's inception in the mid-1990s. In contrast, the 2005 Kaiser Family Foundation and Health Research and Educational Trust (KFF/HRET) annual survey of employer health benefits found that worker contributions to employer-provided family health insurance coverage in 2005 averaged $2,713, a nominal increase of 46 percent over 1996 premiums (Kaiser Family Foundation and Health Research and Educational Trust, 2005). The gap between civilian prices and TRICARE is wider when considering the TRICARE Standard/Extra option (similar to a preferred provider organization, or PPO), which currently requires no premium contribution.

Since service personnel can conceivably retire in their late 30s or early 40s, many of these individuals are working in second careers and have access to non-DoD health insurance. Yet the growing gap between civilian health insurance premiums and TRICARE enrollment fees makes TRICARE an increasingly attractive option vis-à-vis civilian coverage. Recent evidence shows an expansion in the number of civilian employees who decline employer-sponsored health insurance coverage even when it is offered, most likely due to rising civilian insurance premiums (State Health Access Data Center and the Urban Institute, 2006). Recent evidence also suggests that TRICARE beneficiaries are becoming more reliant on DoD health coverage over time. A 2006 Institute for Defense Analyses report finds that utilization of TRICARE benefits increased across all beneficiary groups between 2003 and 2005. For retirees under the age of 65 and their family members, the average annual outpatient resource consumption[1] for beneficiaries with a military primary care manager increased by 17 percent. This increase was even more pronounced for Standard/Extra beneficiaries, among whom average annual outpatient resource consumption increased by 26 percent from 2003 to 2005 (Institute for Defense Analyses, 2006).

In an effort to control escalating health care costs associated with this increased demand, DoD might consider altering the structure of the health care benefits provided to military retirees and their dependents by creating incentives for DoD retirees to choose civilian health insurance. Such incentives could take the form of subsidies or transfers to individuals who choose employer-provided coverage in lieu of TRICARE. However, to understand whether such changes would be optimal from a cost perspective, DoD needs a better understanding of how many beneficiaries have *access* to civilian-provided health insurance coverage—even if they are not currently enrolled in a civilian plan. Further, DoD needs estimates of average health insurance premiums paid by retired beneficiaries with civilian plans and needs to understand the reasons why beneficiaries may (or may not) choose civilian plans over TRICARE. To obtain more concrete information concerning these issues, DoD asked RAND Corporation to conduct a pilot survey of retired beneficiaries under the age of 65. The goals of the survey, the 2005 Survey of Military Retirees (SMR), included the following:

- Estimate the percentage of retirees who are eligible for civilian health insurance, either through their own or their spouse's employment or through a union or professional association.
- Estimate the percentage of retirees enrolled in civilian health insurance plans.
- Explore the reasons for *not* participating in civilian employer health insurance.
- Estimate the premium costs retirees pay to enroll in their civilian health plans.
- Estimate how changes in civilian premiums would affect participation in civilian employer-provided health plans

---

[1] Average annual outpatient resource consumption is measured here using outpatient "relative value units" (RVUs). Instead of just counting the number of patient-physician encounters or the time spent during the encounter, RVUs are a utilization measure of patient-physician encounters that weight each encounter to reflect the physician resources consumed for the services provided during the encounter.

- Estimate the use of TRICARE facilities and benefits by those with in civilian health insurance.

Although existing surveys of DoD beneficiaries provide information on enrollment in TRICARE Prime and on the use of TRICARE Standard/Extra, they do not provide information on the number of retirees who have access to other insurance. Our survey was designed to enhance DoD's knowledge of the civilian health insurance options available to DoD beneficiaries, regardless of whether they enroll in these plans. In addition, our survey provides insight into whether beneficiaries view TRICARE as their primary source of insurance coverage. Understanding the size of the beneficiary population that relies on TRICARE—even if they do not currently use TRICARE—is relevant from an actuarial standpoint. Nonusers who view TRICARE as their primary source of health insurance coverage will pose an actuarial risk if they become unhealthy in the future.

Purpose of This Report

This report attempts to fill the information gap that currently exists regarding civilian health insurance options that retirees have and their reasons for participation or nonparticipation in these plans, along with their reliance on TRICARE. The purpose of this report is primarily descriptive rather than analytical. We present an overview of the survey findings with respect to the survey goals listed above. Follow-on work is aimed at combining the survey responses with other data to assess the implications of benefit design changes on TRICARE usage and costs. For example, one follow-on study is simulating the implications of offering a health savings account to beneficiaries with no civilian insurance. Another is examining the health care status of military retirees and their use of TRICARE versus use of civilian medical care.

The TRICARE System

TRICARE is a nationwide health insurance plan available to active-duty DoD personnel, retirees, and their families and dependents. TRICARE currently offers beneficiaries two primary insurance options—an HMO plan called TRICARE Prime, and a PPO plan available through TRICARE Standard and TRICARE Extra. Although TRICARE Standard and Extra are often described as separate plans, TRICARE Standard represents the "out of network" component of a traditional PPO, and TRICARE Extra represents the "in-network" component. TRICARE Standard is a fee-for-service plan that gives beneficiaries the option to see any TRICARE-certified or authorized provider (e.g., doctor, nurse-practitioner, lab, clinic) and requires that beneficiaries satisfy a yearly deductible before TRICARE cost sharing begins. There are also copayments or cost shares for outpatient care, medications, and inpatient care (Office of the Assistant Secretary of Defense, Health Affairs, and the TRICARE Management Activity, 2006d).

"Standard" offers the greatest flexibility in choosing a provider, but it also involves greater out-of-pocket expenses for the patient. "Extra" goes into effect whenever a Standard beneficiary chooses to make an appointment with a TRICARE network provider. Extra, like Standard, requires no enrollment and involves no enrollment fee. Extra is essentially an option for Standard beneficiaries who want to save on out-of-pocket expenses by seeking care from a TRICARE Prime network provider (e.g., doctor, nurse practitioner, lab). The cost-sharing rate with the in-network provider is 5 percent less than it would be with a doctor who is a nonnetwork TRICARE-authorized or participating provider. In addition, the network provider will generally file all claims forms for the beneficiary and agree not to bill for amounts above TRICARE allowable charges. When using the Extra option, the Standard beneficiary must meet the same requirements to satisfy a deductible and must also pay a cost share for treatment (Office of the Assistant Secretary of Defense, Health Affairs, and the TRICARE Management Activity, 2006c).

Medical services in the TRICARE system are provided either at DoD hospitals called military treatment facilities (MTFs) or through contracts with the civilian sector. Enrollees in TRICARE Prime are assigned a primary care manager (PCM) and agree to seek treatment from their PCM first. Typically, the PCM will be the local MTF, unless the retiree does not live in an MTF catchment area or the local MTF does not have room for new patients (Office of the Assistant Secretary of Defense, Health Affairs, and the TRICARE Management Activity, 2006a). Prime beneficiaries must obtain care from the MTF or through a civilian network provider with PCM referral; this is one reason why some beneficiaries prefer a civilian health plan. As with a traditional HMO, individuals enrolled in TRICARE Prime must confer with and get referrals from a PCM before seeking specialty care. In contrast, users of Standard/Extra can see any provider in the civilian sector without a referral, with the caveat that coinsurance rates for an in-network provider are lower than those for an out-of-network provider. While Standard/Extra users can seek care at an MTF if they choose, retired Prime enrollees are prioritized over retired Standard/Extra users if space at the MTF is limited (Office of the Assistant Secretary of Defense, Health Affairs, and the TRICARE Management Activity, 2006c).

Cost-sharing requirements differ across the two basic TRICARE options and are presented in greater detail in Table 1.1. TRICARE Prime requires a premium contribution of $230 per year for an individual and $460 per year for a family. Although the Standard/Extra options require no premium contribution, users of Standard/Extra must pay a yearly deductible. One cannot directly compare the copayments in TRICARE Prime to the coinsurance rates in Standard/Extra, but in most cases, the coinsurance payments will exceed the $12 outpatient visit fee for civilian visits; MTF visits are free for Prime enrollees.

A comparison of the figures in Table 1.1 with similar civilian statistics available through the KFF/HRET (2004) survey of employees and the Bureau of Labor Statistics' National Compensation Survey (2005) shows that DoD and civilian cost-sharing differentials are most pronounced in terms of premium price. Deductibles, office-visit copays, and catastrophic cap amounts are similar in DoD and civilian plans. The data collected in the current survey focuses primarily on premium contributions, as well as overall reasons for choosing (or not choosing) TRICARE.

Table 1.1
Cost-Sharing Requirements for DoD Retirees and Their Families

Selected Characteristics	HMO Option TRICARE Prime	PPO Option TRICARE Extra (In-Network)	PPO Option TRICARE Standard (Out-of-Network)
Yearly premium	$230 (individual) $460 (family)	$0	$0
Copays or coinsurance (regular office visits)	$12/outpatient civilian visit	20% of negotiated fee	25% of allowed charges
Deductibles	$0	$150 (individual) $300 (family)	$150 (individual) $300 (family)
Family catastrophic caps	$3,000/year	$3,000/year	$3,000/year
Pharmacy copays			
MTF pharmacy	$0 if MTF pharmacy	$0 if MTF pharmacy	$0 if MTF pharmacy
TRICARE mail-order/network retail pharmacy	$3 (generic) $9 (brand name) $22 (nonformulary)	$3 (generic) $9 (brand name) $22 (nonformulary)	$3 (generic) $9 (brand name) $22 (nonformulary)
Nonnetwork retail pharmacy	50%, after $300/person, $600/family deductible	The greater of 20% or $9 (generic or brand name) or $22 (nonformulary) after $150/person, $300/family deductible	The greater of 20% or $9 (generic or brand name) or $22 (nonformulary) after $150/person, $300/family deductible

Pharmacy cost-sharing requirements do not differ across TRICARE options so long as the prescription is filled by an MTF pharmacy, the TRICARE mail-order pharmacy (TMOP), or by retail network pharmacies. Prime enrollees pay a higher percentage cost share at nonnetwork retail pharmacies (see Table 1.1).

Data

We used three main data sources for this report. First, to identify the survey population and select the sample, we used data on retirees and their dependents maintained by DoD. The Defense Enrollment Eligibility Reporting System (DEERS) is a computerized database of military personnel and their families and others who are entitled under the law to TRICARE benefits. DEERS registration is required for TRICARE eligibility. Active-duty and retired service members are automatically registered in DEERS, but they need to enroll their family members to ensure their eligibility for benefits. For example, retail network pharmacies check TRICARE eligibility through DEERS and fill prescriptions only for beneficiaries who are listed as eligible in DEERS. Military personnel are expected to keep the DEERS records updated to reflect changes in personal eligibility information, including changes in military career status, addresses, and family status. We used information from the August 2005 DEERS to identify retired officers and enlisted personnel under age 65 who were living in the continental United States (CONUS) and who had been retired for at least one year (i.e., retired on or before June

30, 2004). This was the survey population from which the sample was selected. Chapter Two provides more details about sample selection.

Second, we used data from the 2003 SMR to obtain estimates of likely response rates and labor-force participation that were used to calculate the needed sample size. The 2003 survey was designed to represent active-duty retirees who retired between January 1, 1971 and December 31, 2001, who were living in the United States or on U.S. military installations overseas (excluding territories), and who were receiving or were eligible to receive retirement pay as of the end of December 2002 (Defense Manpower Data Center, 2004). The survey was fielded between August and October 2003, using a nonproportional, stratified, single-stage random sample of 51,568 retirees, with a weighted response rate of 65 percent. The 2003 SMR focused on attitudes and perceptions related to postservice employment and on earnings of retirees and use of health care, with an emphasis on the effects of combat-related disabilities. Data from the 2003 SMR offered useful background information during the planning phase of the 2005 SMR. For example, as noted in Chapter Two, estimates from the 2003 survey of the percentage of retirees currently in the civilian labor force, cross-tabulated by age and rank, allowed us to develop a sampling method that maximized the anticipated effective sample size of the 2005 survey.

Third, the main data source is the 2005 SMR that we designed and fielded in February–March, 2006. The survey was a computer-assisted telephone interview (CATI) that asked questions about the labor-force participation of the respondent and his or her spouse, eligibility and participation in civilian health insurance options, reasons for participation or nonparticipation, use of TRICARE and other options to pay for medical care, and the likely effect of premium increases or decreases on participation in civilian health insurance plans (if eligible). The total number of respondents was 933, corresponding to a response rate of 59.7 percent.

Organization of the Report

Chapter Two presents details about the survey methodology—the survey population, the sample design, an overview of the survey instrument, and a brief description of the implementation and fielding of the survey. The final section in the chapter shows the overall response rates for the survey and the calculation of the sample weights for the analysis. Chapter Three presents some basic descriptive statistics. These are drawn both from our survey and from the 2003 SMR. In Chapter Four, we discuss accessibility to and eligibility for civilian health insurance. Chapter Five examines participation in civilian health insurance plans. We also provide an estimate of the elasticity of demand for civilian health insurance based on survey questions. Chapter Six examines the use of TRICARE for those with and without access to civilian health insurance plans. Chapter Seven presents conclusions. The survey instrument is included as Appendix A, and Appendix B provides confidence intervals corresponding to the data presented in Chapters Three through Six.

CHAPTER TWO

Survey Methodology, Fielding, and Response Rates

Defining the Survey Population

The survey was meant to be a pilot study to obtain data on a small sample for immediate policy purposes and to develop an instrument that could be used in larger surveys of military retirees to better track their civilian health insurance options and reasons for participation or nonparticipation in those options. As such, all retired service members, officers and enlisted personnel, were eligible for the survey. We used the August 2005 DEERS data file as the sampling frame. Because we were primarily interested in those who were employed in the civilian sector and thus might have access to civilian health insurance, we restricted the survey population in several ways. First, we restricted eligibility to those under 65 years of age and therefore eligible for TRICARE.[1] Second, we restricted eligibility to retirees who had retired during the past 20 years and those who had been retired for at least one year as of August 2005. This was to ensure that retirees were still likely to be in the labor force and also that the most recent retirees would have had sufficient time to enter the labor force. Data from the 2003 SMR indicated that the labor-force participation rate of military retirees declined with age, from over 80 percent for those under 60 to 50 percent for those aged 64 (Figure 2.1). By the last year of regular TRICARE eligibility, only half of military retirees are in the labor force. As we describe below, we took this decline in labor-force participation into account in the sample design.

Thus, the survey population included all active-duty retirees from the Army, Navy, Marine Corps, or Air Force who met the following criteria:

- retired on or before June 30, 2004
- between 34 and 64 years of age as of August 2005
- living in CONUS
- eligible for retirement pay and military health benefits
- not "disability retired" or eligible for Medicare A or B.

A total of 881,125 individuals met those criteria, consisting of 206,908 officers and 674,217 enlisted. Throughout this report, when the terms "officer," "retired officer," "enlisted,"

---

[1] Retirees over age 65 have primary coverage from Medicare and secondary coverage from DoD through the TRICARE for Life plan.

Figure 2.1
Percentage of Retired Military Personnel Employed, by Age, 2003 Survey of Military Retirees

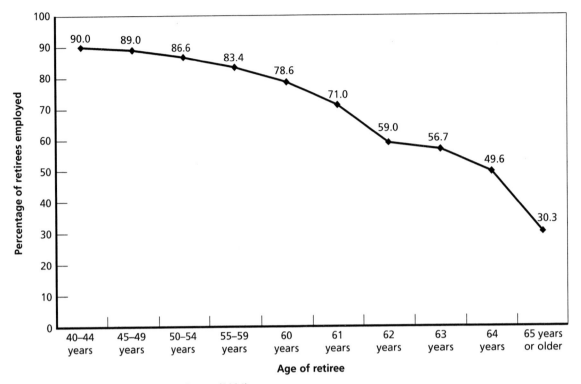

SOURCE: Defense Manpower Data Center (2004).
RAND MG583-2.1

or "retired enlisted" are used, they are used to signify the retired officers and enlisted personnel, respectively, who fit these criteria just described, unless otherwise specified.

Sample Selection

The DEERS data showed that 77 percent of the individuals of interest were retired enlisted personnel. Given the diversity of experience, education, and training, we could not assume that civilian employment opportunities were the same for retired officers and enlisted personnel; thus, it seemed important to be able to disaggregate responses by officer or enlisted. This called for a disproportionate allocation of the overall sample to the officer stratum (i.e., more than 23 percent would need to be allocated to retired officers) to ensure sufficient sample size for developing separate estimates for the two groups.

Given our budget constraints and an estimated overall response rate of 65 percent based on the 2003 SMR, we settled on an overall sample size of 1,600, equally split between officers and enlisted. Given that many survey items would apply only to working military retirees, we sought an optimal balance in the effective sample size of both the total number of retirees and the number of working retirees in our sample. To accomplish this goal, given that the proportion of military retirees who are working begins to tail off after age 60 (see Figure 2.1), we further stratified the retired officer and enlisted classes by age of the retiree, using five strata: 60 years or younger, 61 years, 62 years, 63 years, 64 years. The sample was selected using disproportionate sampling rates within each stratum.[2] Table 2.1 shows the final sample size and its distribution across the strata.

Of the 1,600 cases, 37 were missing contact information, including phone numbers. As such, the sample size was reduced to 1,563 cases.

Survey Instrument

As mentioned, the survey was implemented as a CATI rather than a mail survey. The complexity of the questions regarding insurance options would have made a such a survey questionnaire unwieldy. The survey instrument (see Appendix A), which was programmed into the CATI system, asked specific questions designed to elicit information about (1) employment status and type of employer (size, sector); (2) spouse's employment status and type of employer (size, sector);

Table 2.1
Sample Selection

Stratum	Number in Sample
Officer	
Age ≤ 60 years	633
61 years	60
62 years	52
63 years	34
64 years	21
Total officer	800
Enlisted	
Age ≤ 60 years	682
61 years	36
62 years	35
63 years	28
64 years	19
Total enlisted	800
Total sample	1,600

---

[2] To achieve optimal balance in the effective sample size, the probability of selection for retired officers decreased uniformly by 15 percent for every year in age past 60, so that the probability of selection for those age 64 was 40 percent of those age 60 or less. Similarly, the probability of selection decreased uniformly by 10 percent for retired enlisted personnel, so that the probability of selection for those age 64 was 60 percent of those age 60 or less.

(3) availability, eligibility, and enrollment in civilian health insurance plans offered through own employer, spouse's employer, union or professional association, or purchased directly from an insurance company; (4) reasons for not enrolling in any of these plans if available and eligible for enrollment; (5) annual premiums and annual out-of-pocket expenses if enrolled in civilian plan; (6) use of TRICARE to pay for medical care when participating in civilian health insurance plans; (7) health status of respondent and family member about whom the respondent is most concerned (likely to drive choice of health care coverage); and (8) likelihood of dropping or enrolling in civilian health insurance coverage if premiums increase or decrease by a stated percentage.

Fielding the Survey

Respondents were initially contacted by a written letter. Each respondent was sent a one-page advance notification letter printed on DoD letterhead and signed by a representative from the Office of the Secretary of Defense, Health Affairs. Two weeks later, each respondent was contacted by telephone for the interview. Calls to respondents began on Monday, January 30, 2006, and ended on Thursday, March 23, 2006. Interviews were conducted by trained interviewers using a programmed CATI instrument.

Tracking

Tracking of respondents was conducted throughout the data collection period. Respondents were tracked if (1) an advance notification letter was returned as undeliverable, (2) an interviewer learned that the telephone number was wrong, (3) a telephone number was disconnected, or (4) an interviewer learned that the respondent had moved. The tracking team utilized a mixture of directory assistance phone calls, Internet searches, and Lexis-Nexis queries to track respondents.

Interview Time

Completed interviews averaged 25 minutes, including the time taken to introduce the survey and gain informed consent. The median time was 22 minutes, the minimum was 6 minutes, and the maximum was 105 minutes.

Level of Effort

It took an average of five calls to complete an interview. The minimum number of calls to complete an interview was one and the maximum was 33. Unless respondents set appointments or asked for callbacks, interviewers stopped calling respondents after 15 unsuccessful attempts (to qualify as an attempt, a call had to be made on a different day and shift from the previous call).

Final Disposition of All Cases

Table 2.2 summarizes the final disposition for all cases in the sample.

Table 2.2
Final Disposition of Sample

Disposition	Number	Percentage
Complete	933	59.7
Refusal to confirm phone number	25	1.6
Respondent refusal	159	10.2
Refusal by other in household	40	2.6
Break-off	9	0.6
Dead	2	0.1
Ill/incapable	2	0.1
Respondent language problem	2	0.1
Respondent away for field period	14	0.9
Ineligible	8	0.5
Reached maximum number of calls	117	7.5
Field period ended	165	10.6
Wrong number	41	2.6
Number was a computer/fax line	8	0.5
Phone number not in service	23	1.5
Unpublished number	15	1.0
Total	1,563	100.0

Survey Response Rates

The unadjusted overall response rate for the sample was 933/1,563 = 59.7 percent.[3] The response rate varied by officer or enlisted and by age, as shown in Table 2.3. Overall, 68 percent of the officers responded to the survey, compared with only 51 percent of the enlisted personnel.

Methodological Notes

The sample observations were weighted, using probability of selection and post-stratification weighting, to account for the differential probability of selection produced by the sample's

---

[3] The Council of American Survey Research Organizations (1982) recommends that for surveys involving a single stage with screening, the response rate should be calculated as follows: the screening completion rate, i.e., the proportion of units in which a decision has been reached about whether or not a unit is eligible multiplied by the interview completion rate; that is, the proportion of screened eligible respondents who completed an interview. In our study, we had a 99-percent screening completion rate if we exclude all cases with refusal to confirm phone number: wrong number, computer line (the number was for a dial-up or fax line—see also table above), not in service, and unpublished number. If we remove the ineligible cases (ten cases total—two deceased and eight coded as ineligible, as shown in Table 2.2), we would have an interview completion rate of 60.1 percent (933/1,553). Thus, the overall response rate is 99 percent * 60.1 percent = 59.5 percent, which is slightly smaller than the unadjusted overall response rate reported above of 59.7 percent.

stratified design and to take into account the differential response rates among the strata, so that the percentages we report here from the survey are weighted to represent the survey population. For example, because retired officers responded at a higher rate than retired enlisted personnel (see Table 2.3), we apply a higher post-stratification weight to the enlisted responses when calculating estimates of the full population of retirees. The sampling design and survey weights were taken into consideration in all calculations of variability when generalizing to the survey population.

While the total number of respondents is 933, the number of responses available for analysis drops as the data is parsed into important subsets, such as officer and enlisted, retirees with and without families, those eligible to enroll in a civilian plan, and those actually enrolled in such a plan. Thus, the level of precision in the estimates presented fluctuates as we progress through the survey results, and it is important to individually note the margins of error associated with estimates of the sample population.

As a measure of the uncertainty surrounding the estimate, we report the lower and upper bounds of the 95-percent confidence interval around the estimated population mean or proportion,[4] typically written in parentheses with a comma separating the lower and upper bounds. This does not imply that the interval contains the population parameter with certainty; simply

Table 2.3
Response Rates, by Stratum

Stratum	Number in Sample	Number of Completes	Response Rate (percentage)
Officer			
Age ≤ 60 years	625	424	67.8
61 years	54	37	68.5
62 years	51	36	70.6
63 years	31	22	71.0
64 years	18	11	61.1
Total officer	779	530	68.0
Enlisted			
Age ≤ 60 years	668	339	50.8
61 years	35	20	57.1
62 years	34	18	52.9
63 years	28	16	57.1
64 years	19	10	52.6
Total enlisted	784	403	51.4
Total sample	1,563	933	59.7

---

[4]   The confidence interval for means or proportions is calculated as [estimate ± ($t_{.025}$ * standard error)], where $t_{.025}$ represents the 97.5th percentile of Student's t distribution, with the appropriate degrees of freedom.

that in repeated sampling, the procedure will contain the true population parameter 95 percent of the time. Confidence interval estimates for survey results may be found in the figure or table accompanying the result or embedded within the text describing the result. Confidence intervals in figures are displayed as vertical lines; for each figure, a corresponding table with numerical interval estimates may be found in Appendix B.

As mentioned previously, given the diversity of experience, education, and training, we could not assume that civilian employment opportunities are the same for retired officers and enlisted personnel; thus, it seemed important to be able to disaggregate responses by officer or enlisted. It is not the intention of this report to test for systematic differences between retired officers and enlisted personnel, but rather to summarize the health care information collected in the survey for each group. As such, we do not routinely test for statistical differences between the two groups (or between other natural groupings presented), except in those cases specified in the text for which the contrast was of particular interest.

CHAPTER THREE

Profile of Military Retirees

This chapter provides a descriptive profile of the population of military retirees who are under age 65, living in CONUS, eligible for military benefits, and who did not receive a disability discharge.

The 2005 DEERS data provide an overview of the population in terms of gender, age, and labor-force status. Overall, about 93 percent of the population consisted of men. The percentage of women was a little higher in the retired enlisted population (8 percent) than in the officer population (6 percent). Figure 3.1 shows the distribution of the survey population by age. About 70 percent of officers and 80 percent of enlisted were 60 years or younger, and as we show below, very likely to be employed full time in the civilian labor force.

Figure 3.1
Distribution of Retired Officers and Enlisted Personnel in the Survey Population, by Age, 2005

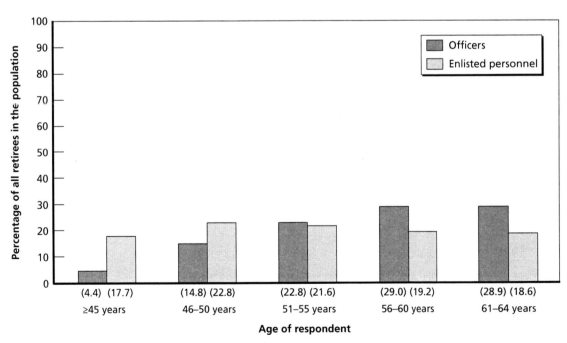

RAND *MG583-3.1*

We now turn to our survey findings. Several points should be noted:

- All data reported here are weighted estimates from the survey.
- We report separate estimates for officers and enlisted personnel.
- We group together those ages 61–64 years because small sample sizes in these strata do not allow enough statistical precision to identify meaningful differences in respondents' answers among individual years of age in this range.
- 95-percent confidence intervals are provided for each estimate, either in the form of error bars in figures or included in parentheses in tables. For figures, the actual intervals are provided in corresponding tables in Appendix B.

Employment Status of Retirees

Overall, about 80 (77.1, 83.0) percent of the survey population was employed. About 78 (74.5, 81.8) percent of officers and 81 (76.9, 84.4) percent of enlisted personnel were employed. Respondents were asked whether they were not working because of a disability. While the overall percentage of retirees who reported not being able to work because of a disability was quite small, 3.2 (1.7, 4.7) percent, a higher percentage of enlisted personnel, 3.6 (1.6, 5.5) percent, than officers, 1.9 (0.8, 3.0) percent, were not working because of a disability.

As expected, the employment rate differed by age (Figure 3.2), but there was no statistical

Figure 3.2
Percentage of Military Retirees Who Were Employed, by Age Group, February–March 2006

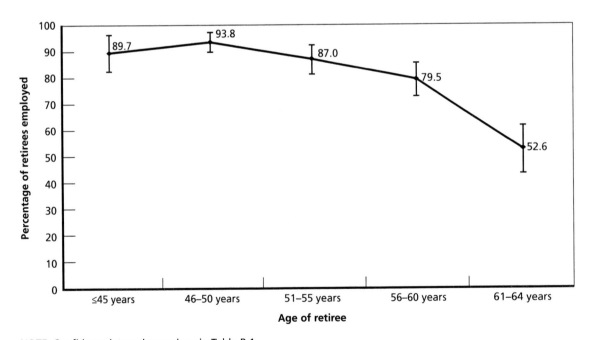

NOTE: Confidence intervals are given in Table B.1.
RAND *MG583-3.2*

difference between officers and enlisted personnel. About 90 percent of those 50 years or younger were employed, as were 87 percent of those ages 51–55 years and 80 percent of those ages 56–60 years. However, these differences were not statistically significant, so in the discussions that follow, we often choose to combine these age groups. Overall, about 87 percent of retirees age 60 years or younger were employed, compared with 53 percent of those between 61 and 64 years.

Between 40 and 50 percent of all retired military were private-sector employees, and a little over one-fifth worked for the government, the majority of whom worked for the federal government (Figure 3.3). About 11 percent of officers and 5 percent of enlisted were self-employed. A small percentage reported working for more than one employer (generally in the private sector and self-employment), although two employers of the same type were possible.

Figure 3.3
Distribution of Retired Officers and Enlisted Personnel, by Employment Status and Type of Employer, February–March 2006

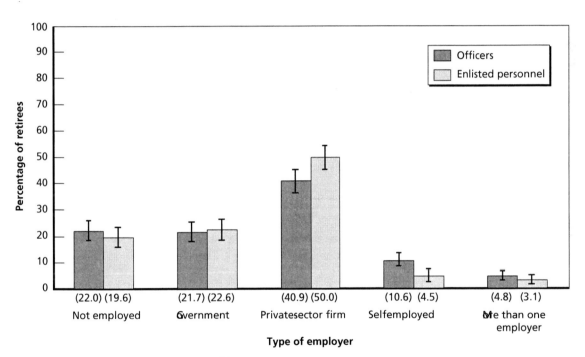

NOTE: Confidence intervals are given in Table B.2.
RAND *MG583-3.3*

Of those who were employed, 90 percent or more of those age 60 or younger were working full time (defined as 35 hours or more per week), compared with 69 percent (enlisted) to 74 percent (officers) of those aged 61–64 (Figure 3.4). Half of the employed 64-year-olds were employed full time.

Figure 3.4
Percentage of Employed Retired Officers and Enlisted Personnel Who Were Working Full Time, by Age Group, February–March 2006

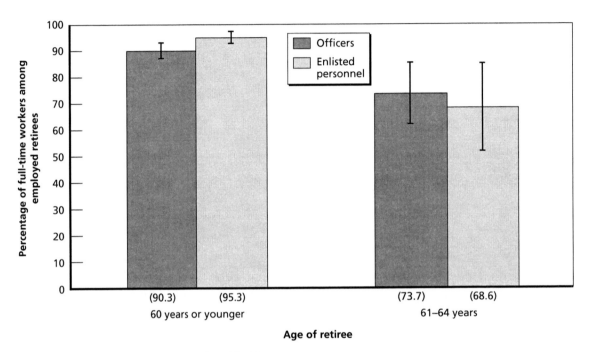

NOTE: Confidence intervals are given in Table B.3.
RAND *MG583-3.4*

Well over half of the retirees who were employed were working for large employers, with 500 or more employees (Figure 3.5). Between 30 and 33 percent worked for employers with fewer than 200 employees. As expected, the majority of self-employed retirees were in the smallest category, although some reported working for large firms (presumably as contractors or consultants, or perhaps as business owners). The size of the firm is important because, as we show later, the smallest firms (with fewer than 50 employees) are least likely to offer health insurance.

Figure 3.5
Distribution of Employed Retired Officers and Enlisted Personnel, by Size of Employer, February–March 2006

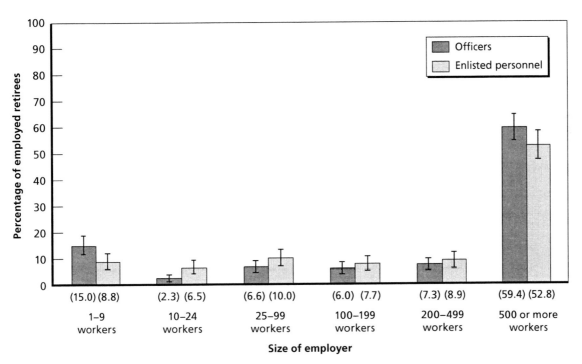

NOTES: Percentages do not add to 100 because a small percentage reported they did not know or were uncertain of the size of the employer. Confidence intervals are given in Table B.4.
RAND *MG583-3.5*

Marital Status and Employment Status of Spouse

Well over four-fifths of the military retirees were currently married and living with their spouse—85 (85.0, 91.1) percent of enlisted personnel and 88 (80.9, 88.0) percent of officers. About 3 (1.6, 4.5) percent had never been married; the remainder were separated, divorced, or widowed.

Figure 3.6 shows the distribution of spouses by employment status as of February–March 2006, and by type of employer. About 46 percent of spouses of officers and 38 percent of enlisted spouses were not employed. About 16–17 percent were employed by the government. Twenty-nine percent of officer spouses and 39 percent of enlisted spouses worked for private firms.

Figure 3.6
Distribution of Spouses of Retired Officers and Enlisted Personnel, by Employment Status and Type of Employer, February–March 2006

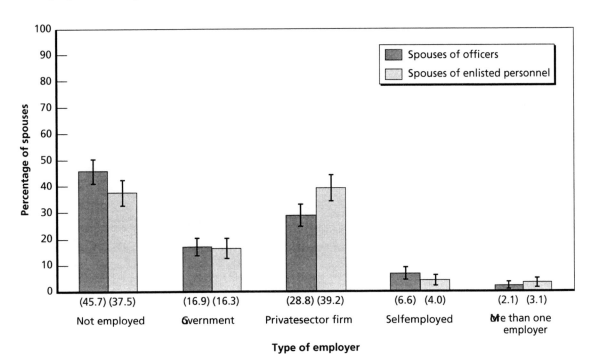

NOTE: Confidence intervals are given in Table B.5.
RAND *MG583-3.6*

Figure 3.7 shows that among employed spouses, about half worked for large firms (with 500 or more workers), while between 19 and 27 percent worked for very small firms (with fewer than 25 workers). Most of the employed spouses worked full time at their jobs—about 71 (65.7, 77.1) percent of officer spouses and 81 (75.6, 85.6) percent of enlisted spouses.

Overall, 13 (10.7, 15.9) percent of retired military households had no one employed in the civilian labor force, 40 (36.3, 44.0) percent had one wage earner (most often the military retiree in married households), and 47 (42.9, 50.2) percent had two wage earners.

Figure 3.7
Distribution of Employed Spouses of Retired Officers and Enlisted Personnel, by Size of Employer, February–March 2006

NOTES: Percentages do not add to 100 because a small percentage reported that they did not know or were uncertain of the size of their spouse's employer. Confidence intervals are given in Table B.6.
RAND *MG583-3.7*

Number of Dependents

Respondents were asked about the number of dependents who were currently eligible for retiree medical benefits under TRICARE, not counting their spouse/partner. The responses were remarkably similar across officers and enlisted personnel. A large majority reported not having any dependents eligible for TRICARE benefits (62–65 percent), and another 30 percent reported having one to two dependents eligible for medical benefits (Figure 3.8).

To get a more accurate picture of the number of family members eligible for TRICARE benefits, we need to add in the spouse if the respondent was married. Eight (6.0, 10.4) percent of the survey population had no family members eligible for TRICARE benefits, 59 (55.7, 63.2) percent of the population had at least one family member, 14 (11.4, 16.7) percent had two family members, and 18 (15.5, 21.2) percent had three or more family members eligible for TRICARE.

Figure 3.8
Percentage of Retired Officers and Enlisted Personnel, by Number of Dependents Eligible for TRICARE Benefits, February–March 2006

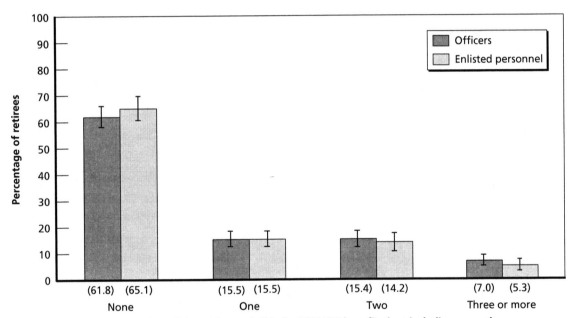

NOTE: Confidence intervals are given in Table B.7.

Annual Household Income

Figure 3.9 shows the distribution of household income of retired military personnel by rank and employment status of the retired individual.[1]

Not surprisingly, the distribution of income for those employed at the time of the survey is skewed higher than the income distribution of those not working. Among those working, two-thirds of retired officers had household incomes of more than $100,000, compared with 18 percent of retired enlisted. About 6 percent of officers and 26 percent of enlisted reported incomes of $50,000 or below. The median income of those employed was over $100,000 for officers and between $50,001 and $75,000 for enlisted.

Among those not working, only 28 percent of retired officers and 7 percent of retired enlisted had incomes of over $100,000, while 22 percent of retired officers and 62 percent of retired enlisted had incomes of $50,000 or less. The median income range was $50,001–$75,000 for officers and $25,001–$50,000 for enlisted.

Chapter Four examines the availability of civilian health insurance to military retirees.

Figure 3.9
Percentage of Retired Officers and Enlisted Personnel, by Annual Household Income and Employment Status, February–March 2006

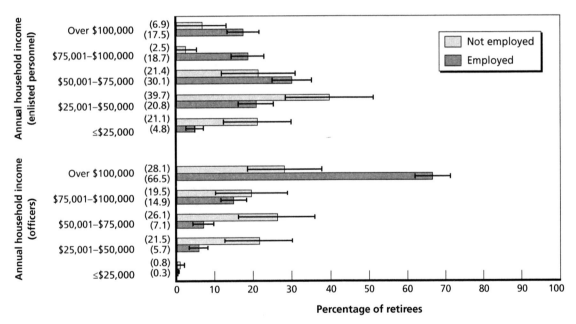

NOTES: Percentages do not add to 100 because 4–8 percent of retirees refused to answer the question or reported that they did not know. Confidence intervals are given in Table B.8.
RAND MG583-3.9

---

[1] Household income includes income from work performed at any job, including bonuses, overtime, tips and commissions, or other compensation, such as retirement pay or unemployment earned by all household members over the age of 15, before taxes.

Eligibility of Military Retirees for Civilian Health Insurance

Respondents were asked a series of questions designed to elicit information about the availability of civilian health insurance options—from their own employer, their spouse's employer (if the respondent was married), and from other civilian sources such as professional or trade associations. In addition, respondents were asked about the eligibility of their spouse and dependents to enroll in such plans.

Sources of Civilian Health Insurance

Tables 4.1 through 4.3 show the percentage of retirees who had access to civilian health insurance through different sources. The tables show two sets of statistics—the first calculated for the relevant group (for example, only those employed are eligible for employer-provided insurance plans, so the relevant group is those employed, as shown in Table 4.1); the second was calculated for the entire population. The latter set is important if we want to speak broadly of what proportion of retirees has access to civilian health insurance and is enrolled in such plans.

Of the 80 percent of retirees who were employed, about 82 percent were eligible to enroll in a plan offered by their current employer, and almost all of them reported that their spouse and/or dependents were also eligible to enroll in such plans (see Table 4.1). The small differences between enlisted and officers are not statistically significant. Overall, of the survey population of military retirees, about 65 percent was eligible for employer-provided insurance and 58 percent of the population was eligible to enroll family members in such plans.

In Chapter Three, we showed that about 61 percent of the survey population had spouses who were employed. Close to 70 percent of retirees with employed spouses reported that their spouse's employer offered civilian health insurance (see Table 4.2). Of these, about 89 percent reported that they and/or their dependents were eligible to enroll in the plan offered by the spouse's employer. As a percentage of the population of military retirees, somewhat over a third—36 percent—had spouses with access to employer-provided civilian health insurance; overall, a little over 30 percent of the population had access to such insurance for themselves and/or their dependents.

Table 4.1
Percentage of Retired Officers and Enlisted Personnel with Access to Civilian Health Insurance Through Own Employer-Provided Insurance

Own Employer-Provided Insurance	Officers	Enlisted	Total
	Percentage 95% confidence interval (lower bound, upper bound)		
Percentage of population employed	78.2 (74.5, 81.8)	80.6 (76.9, 84.4)	80.1 (77.1, 83.0)
Of those employed:			
Respondent eligible to enroll in plan offered by current employer	77.5 (73.4, 81.6)	83.9 (79.9, 88.0)	82.4 (79.2, 85.7)
Of those eligible:			
Eligible to enroll spouse/dependents in plan offered by current employer	98.4 (97.1, 99.8)	96.4 (94.2, 98.7)	95.1 (95.1, 98.7)
Of population:			
Respondent eligible to enroll in plan offered by current employer	60.6 (56.5, 64.6)	66.7 (62.3, 71.1)	65.2 (61.7, 68.7)
Eligible to enroll spouse/ dependents in plan offered by current employer	56.0 (51.9, 60.2)	58.7 (54.0, 63.3)	58.0 (54.4, 61.7)

Table 4.2
Percentage of Retired Officers and Enlisted Personnel with Access to Civilian Health Insurance Through Spouse's Employer-Provided Insurance

Spouse Employer-Provided Insurance	Officers	Enlisted	Total
	Percentage 95% confidence interval (lower bound, upper bound)		
Percentage of population with employed spouses	49.4 (45.0, 53.8)	54.5 (49.8, 59.2)	53.3 (49.5, 57.1)
Of employed spouses:			
Spouse eligible to enroll in plan offered by his/her current employer	60.6 (54.5, 66.6)	71.8 (66.0, 77.6)	69.3 (64.6, 74.1)
Of those eligible:			
Respondent and dependents eligible to enroll in spouse's plan	89.0 (83.8, 94.1)	88.6 (83.4, 93.9)	88.7 (84.3, 93.1)
Of population:			
Spouse eligible to enroll in plan offered by his/her current employer	29.6 (25.7, 33.5)	38.4 (33.8, 43.1)	36.4 (32.7, 40.0)
Respondent and dependents eligible to enroll in spouse's plan	24.9 (21.2, 28.7)	33.0 (28.5, 37.4)	31.1 (27.6, 34.6)

Only about 16 percent of the population reported eligibility for health insurance through another civilian source, such as through a union or professional association (see Table 4.3). There was no difference in the percentage of officer and enlisted personnel with respect to eligibility for such insurance. Of this group, over 90 percent of the retirees were eligible to enroll in such plans and 88 percent could enroll spouses in such plans. However, only about 64 percent could enroll dependents in these plans. Overall, about 14 percent of military retirees were eligible to enroll in plans offered through civilian sources other than employers, and 11 percent could enroll spouses. Only 3 percent of the population could enroll dependents in such plans.

Table 4.3
Percentage of Retired Officers and Enlisted Personnel with Access to Civilian Health Insurance Through Other Civilian Sources

Other Civilian Sources (e.g., union, professional association)	Officers	Enlisted	Total
	Percentage 95% confidence interval (lower bound, upper bound)		
Percentage with access to health insurance plan through other civilian source	16.3 (12.8, 19.8)	15.5 (11.9, 19.1)	15.7 (12.8, 18.6)
Of those eligible:			
Respondent eligible to enroll in plan	98.9 (96.8, 100.0)	91.7 (84.4, 98.9)	93.4 (87.9, 98.9)
Spouse eligible to enroll in plan	87.5 (80.3, 94.6)	88.5 (79.6, 97.4)	88.3 (81.3, 95.2)
Dependents eligible to enroll in plan	38.4 (19.2, 57.5)	70.0 (49.1, 90.9)	63.7 (46.6, 80.8)
Of population:			
Respondent eligible to enroll in plan	15.2 (11.9, 18.5)	13.3 (9.9, 16.6)	13.7 (11.1, 16.4)
Spouse eligible to enroll in plan	11.7 (8.7, 14.7)	11.1 (8.0, 14.2)	11.2 (8.8, 13.7)
Dependents eligible to enroll in plan	1.5 (0.4, 2.6)	3.4 (1.6, 5.1)	2.9 (1.6, 4.3)

Figure 4.1 presents the distribution of retirees by the sources of civilian insurance to which they have access. Figure 4.2 presents the same information for families but includes only retirees with families. Because there is no statistical difference between access of officers and enlisted personnel, we show only the population totals. Of course, all the retirees are eligible for TRICARE coverage.

Overall, looking at retirees, we find that about 24 percent of the survey population did not have access to any other source of health insurance for themselves. The most common sources of health insurance were through their own employer (36 percent) and through both their and their spouse's employer (21 percent). Much smaller percentages were eligible only through their spouse's employer (6 percent), non-employer sources (4 percent), a combination of their own employer and non-employer sources (5 percent), their spouse's employer, and another source (less than 1 percent). About 5 percent had access for self-coverage through all three sources (own employer, spouse's employer, non-employer source).

Figure 4.1
Percentage of Military Retirees with Access to Different Sources of Civilian Health Insurance for Self-Coverage, February–March 2006

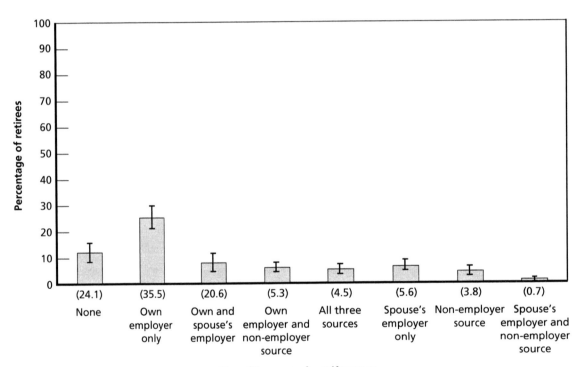

NOTE: Confidence intervals are given in Table B.9.

RAND *MG583-4.1*

Figure 4.2
Percentage of Military Retirees with Families with Access to Different Sources of Civilian Health Insurance for Family Coverage, February–March 2006

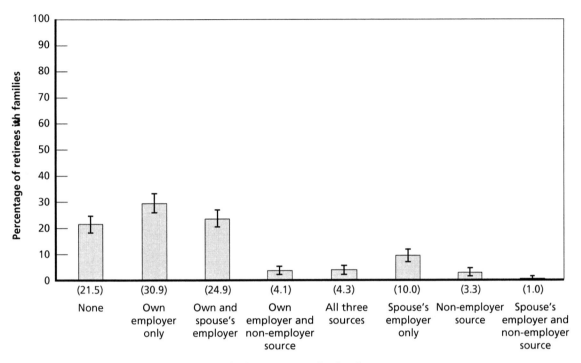

NOTE: Confidence intervals are given in Table B.9.
RAND *MG583-4.2*

Among retirees with families, 22 percent did not have access to family coverage other than through TRICARE. About 31 percent had access to family coverage through their own employer, 25 percent through both their own and their spouse's employer, and 10 percent through their spouse's employer only.

Overall, if we count all sources of coverage for either the retiree or their families, we find that 27 (23.2, 31.0) percent of officers and 21 (16.8, 24.8) percent of enlisted personnel (22 [19.1, 25.5] percent of the survey population) reported not having access to any other form of health insurance for themselves and/or their families.

Prevalence of Incentives Not to Enroll in Employer-Provided Plans

Anecdotal evidence had suggested that some employers were targeting employees who were eligible for TRICARE and offering explicit incentives not to enroll in employer-provided insurance plans, presumably in an effort to reduce employer costs of providing benefits. To examine the prevalence of such incentives, we asked military retirees who had access to employer-provided insurance plans either through their own employer or through their spouse's, whether the employer offered such incentives and whether these were particularly targeted to TRICARE-eligible employees. Table 4.4 presents the responses.

Table 4.4
Percentage of Retired Officers and Enlisted Personnel Offered Incentives Not to Enroll in Employer-Provided Health Insurance Plans

Employer-Provided Insurance	Officers	Enlisted	Total
	Percentage 95% confidence interval (lower bound, upper bound)		
Own employer-provided insurance			
Of those eligible to enroll in plan offered by own employer:			
Employer offered explicit incentive not to enroll in plan	10.2 (7.0, 13.4)	11.7 (7.8, 15.6)	11.4 (8.3, 14.5)
Of those offered incentive not to enroll:			
Incentive not to enroll was specific to TRICARE-eligible employees	21.5 (7.0, 36.0)	9.2 (0.0, 19.5)	11.4 (2.5, 20.2)
Of population:			
Employer offered explicit incentive not to enroll in plan	6.2 (4.2, 8.1)	7.9 (5.3, 10.6)	7.5 (5.4, 9.6)
Incentive not to enroll was specific to TRICARE-eligible employees	1.2 (0.3, 2.1)	0.7 (0.0, 1.5)	0.8 (0.2, 1.5)
Spouse's employer-provided insurance			
Of those with spouses eligible to enroll in plan offered by spouse's employer:			
Employer offered explicit incentive not to enroll in plan	6.8 (2.9, 10.7)	7.6 (3.1, 12.1)	7.5 (3.8, 11.2)
Of those offered incentive not to enroll:			
Incentive not to enroll was specific to TRICARE-eligible employees	8.9 (0.0, 27.6)	0.0 —	1.5 (0.0, 4.8)
Of population:			
Employer offered explicit incentive not to enroll in plan	1.9 (0.8, 3.1)	2.8 (1.2, 4.5)	2.6 (1.3, 3.9)
Incentive not to enroll was specific to TRICARE-eligible employees	0.2 (0.0, 0.5)	0.0 —	0.0 (0.0, 0.1)

About 11 percent of those working and eligible for an employer-provided insurance plan had been offered such incentives, and about one-tenth (11 percent) of this group reported that the incentive was specific to TRICARE-eligible employees. As a percentage of the population, this constituted a very small percentage—less than 8 percent were offered incentives not to enroll in civilian employer insurance plans, and less than 1 percent reported that this was specific to TRICARE-eligible employees. About 8 percent of employers of spouses offered incentives not to use employer-provided health insurance, and less than 2 percent of those targeted TRICARE-eligible employees. Overall, about 3 percent of spouses' employers offered incentives not to enroll, and the percentage that targeted TRICARE-eligible employees specifically was essentially zero.

If we assume that respondents and spouses were not employed by the same employers, across the population, about 11 percent of military retirees were offered incentives by either their own or their spouse's employers not to enroll in civilian insurance plans, and about 1 percent reported that such incentives were specific to TRICARE-eligible employees.

Employers Providing Civilian Health Insurance

The provision of employer-provided health benefits is likely to vary by size and type of employer and by whether the person is working full or part time and, sometimes, by how long the person has worked for the employer. The annual surveys conducted by KFF/HRET of private and public employers of three or more workers provide considerable data on employer-provided health benefits (Kaiser Family Foundation and Health Research and Educational Trust, 2005). Some relevant findings from the 2004 and 2005 KFF/HRET surveys include the following:

- The percentage of firms offering health benefits has declined over time, from 69 percent in 2000 to 60 percent in 2005. This drop is largely because of a decline in the percentage of small firms (with 3–199 workers) offering coverage, which fell from 68 percent in 2000 to 59 percent in 2005.
- The 2004 survey showed that fewer than one-quarter of all firms offered health benefits to part-time workers and larger firms were more likely than smaller firms to do so. For example, while 20 percent of firms with 3–24 workers offered benefits to part-time workers, half or more of large firms (with 1,000 or more workers) did so. Coverage for part-time workers was also more prevalent in firms with smaller percentages of part-time workers (less than 25 percent).
- The likelihood that a firm offers health benefits to its workers varies considerably with the firm's characteristics, such as firm size, the proportion of part-time workers in the firm, and whether workers are unionized. For example,
  - In 2005, only 47 percent of the smallest firms (with fewer than 10 workers) offered health benefits, compared with 72 percent of firms with 10–24 workers, 87 percent of those with 25–49 workers, and over 90 percent of firms with 50 or more workers.
  - In 2004, almost all firms with union workers (96 percent) offered health benefits, compared with 61 percent of firms that did not have union employees.

We used the data from our survey on the type and size of employers and whether the respondent (and spouse, where relevant) worked full or part time to examine whether the trends were the same. Figure 4.3, which shows the relationship between firm size and the provision of health insurance, reinforces the findings of the national KFF/HRET survey. Respondents working for smaller firms were much more likely to report that they were not eligible for employer-provided health insurance. Only 23 percent of those working in firms with fewer than 10 workers, and 61 percent of those in firms with 10–25 workers, had access to such insurance, compared with over 90 percent of those working for firms with 25 workers or more. The small dip in insurance offer rates of firms with 200–499 workers is statistically insignificant.

Figure 4.3
Percentage of Military Retirees Reporting Eligibility for Employer Health Insurance, by Size of Employer, February–March 2006

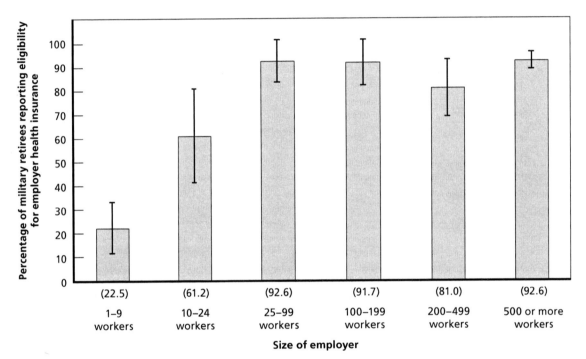

NOTE: Confidence intervals are given in Table B.10.
RAND *MG583-4.3*

Figure 4.4 examines the differences in insurance offer rates by type of employer. As expected, almost all those who worked for the government (97 percent) had access to health insurance, compared with 85 percent of those who worked for private firms. Only 21 percent of those who reported being self-employed had access to health insurance. About 68 percent of those with more than one employer had access to health insurance.

Not surprisingly, there was a very large difference in the percentage of those offered health insurance, depending on whether they worked full or part time, mirroring what the KFF/HRET study showed. While 88 (85.4, 91.2) percent of those working full time had access to employer-provided health insurance, only 27 (9.4, 44.5) percent of those working between 20 and 35 hours and 17 (0.0, 37.1) percent of those working fewer than 20 hours were eligible for such insurance.

Figure 4.4
Percentage of Military Retirees Reporting Eligibility for Employer Health Insurance, by Type of Employer, February–March 2006

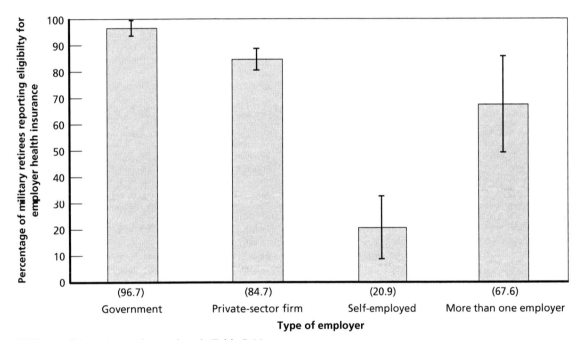

NOTE: Confidence intervals are given in Table B.11.
RAND *MG583-4.4*

CHAPTER FIVE

Participation of Military Retirees in Civilian Health Care Plans

This chapter examines the participation of military retirees and their families in civilian health care plans, reasons for their participation or nonparticipation, and the annual premiums for enrollment in civilian plans. It also reports on the distribution of out-of-pocket costs. Chapter Six examines the use of TRICARE, civilian plans, and other coverage for the provision of medical care and to pay for prescription drugs.

Enrollment in Civilian Health Insurance Plans

Apart from those plans for which they might be eligible through their own or their spouse's employer or professional association, all retirees have access to insurance that could be purchased directly from an insurance company and to care provided through the VA. In addition, some may have access to short-term coverage under the provisions of the Consolidated Omnibus Budget Reconciliation Act (COBRA) because of a job change.[1] The survey asked retirees about all these sources of insurance and whether they and their families were enrolled in any of these plans. The responses are shown in Table 5.1.

Looking first at self-coverage for the retiree, we find that overall, about 40 percent of military retirees with access to their own employer-provided insurance for self-coverage enrolled in such plans, and about 20 percent enrolled in a plan provided by their spouse's employer (officers had slightly higher enrollment rates than enlisted personnel). About 24 percent of officers with access to insurance through a professional association or union enrolled in such plans for self-coverage, compared with only 12 percent of enlisted personnel, but the difference was not statistically significant.

Turning now to family coverage, we find that, interestingly, families were much more likely to be enrolled in the spouse's employer plan (approximately 45 percent) than in the one provided

---

[1]   Congress passed the landmark Consolidated Omnibus Budget Reconciliation Act (COBRA) health benefit provisions in 1986. The law amends the Employee Retirement Income Security Act, the Internal Revenue Code, and the Public Health Service Act to provide continuation of group health coverage that otherwise might be terminated. COBRA provides certain former employees, retirees, spouses, former spouses, and dependent children the right to temporary continuation of health coverage at group rates when coverage is lost due to certain specific events. Group health coverage for COBRA participants is usually more expensive than health coverage for active employees, since the employer usually pays a part of the premium for active employees while COBRA participants generally pay the entire premium themselves. It is ordinarily less expensive, though, than individual health coverage (U.S. Department of Labor, undated).

Table 5.1
Percentage of Retired Officers and Enlisted Personnel and Spouse/Dependents Enrolled in Civilian Health Insurance Plans

Types of Civilian Health Insurance	Officers		Enlisted Personnel		Total Population	
	Retirees	Spouse/ Dependents	Retirees	Spouse/ Dependents	Retirees	Spouse/ Dependents
	Estimate 95% confidence intervals (lower bound, upper bound)					
Of those with access to specific insurance:						
Own employer-provided	41.6 (36.3, 46.8)	33.8 (28.5, 39.0)	39.2 (33.3, 45.0)	28.2 (22.4, 33.9)	39.7 (35.0, 44.4)	29.4 (24.9, 34.0)
Spouse employer-provided	23.7 (16.3, 31.2)	43.0 (35.3, 50.8)	19.1 (12.3, 25.9)	45.0 (36.9, 53.1)	20.0 (14.3, 25.6)	44.6 (38.0, 51.3)
Provided through union/professional association	24.0 (13.7, 34.4)	34.0 (20.2, 47.8)	12.4 (4.3, 20.6)	11.1 (1.7, 20.4)	15.5 (8.9, 21.0)	16.7 (9.0, 24.4)
Of population:						
Own employer-provided	25.4 (21.7, 29.2)	19.0 (15.7, 22.3)	26.2 (21.9, 30.5)	16.6 (13.0, 20.2)	26.0 (22.6, 29.4)	17.2 (14.3, 20.0)
Spouse employer-provided	5.9 (3.9, 8.0)	12.7 (9.7, 15.7)	6.3 (3.9, 8.7)	17.3 (13.6, 21.0)	6.2 (4.4, 8.1)	16.2 (13.3, 19.1)
Provided through union/professional association	3.7 (1.8, 5.7)	4.1 (2.1, 6.1)	1.7 (0.5, 2.9)	1.3 (0.2, 2.4)	2.2 (1.3, 3.2)	1.9 (1.0, 2.9)
Purchased directly from insurance company	3.8 (2.1, 5.5)	4.5 (2.7, 6.4)	1.9 (0.6, 3.2)	2.2 (0.8, 3.6)	2.4 (1.3, 3.4)	2.7 (1.6, 3.9)
Provided by VA	10.9 (8.2, 13.7)	0.8 (0.1, 1.6)	21.9 (17.8, 26.0)	4.3 (2.3, 6.3)	19.3 (16.1, 22.5)	3.5 (1.9, 5.3)
Other non-TRICARE sources (e.g., COBRA)	3.4 (1.8, 5.1)	6.2 (4.1, 8.3)	2.9 (1.2, 4.7)	4.8 (2.6, 6.9)	3.1 (1.7, 4.4)	5.1 (3.4, 6.8)

Figure 5.1
Percentage of Retired Officers and Enlisted Personnel Enrolled in Civilian Health Insurance Plans for Self-Coverage, February–March 2006

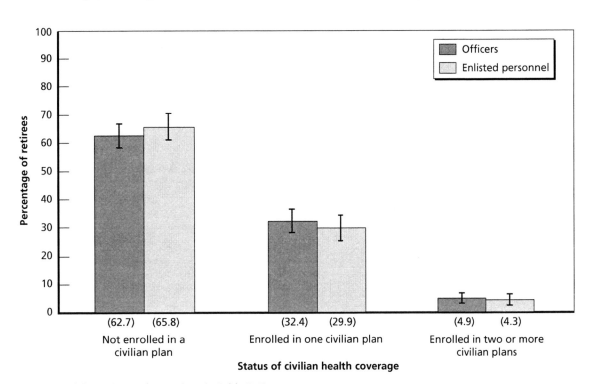

NOTE: Confidence intervals are given in Table B.12.
RAND *MG583-5.1*

by retirees' employers for which they were eligible. Part of this may be because spouses may choose to be enrolled in their own plan, particularly if it is offered for free. Officers were much more likely to enroll their spouse/dependents in the plan available through a professional association (34 percent), compared with enlisted personnel.

As a percentage of the total population, a little over one-quarter of the retirees were enrolled in their own employer-provided plan, 6 percent were enrolled in their spouse's employer-provided plans, and 2 percent were enrolled in plans offered through professional associations or unions. Very few purchased health insurance directly through insurance companies (4 percent of officers and 2 percent of enlisted personnel). About 11 percent of officers and 22 percent of enlisted personnel took advantage of coverage offered by the VA. Overall, about 3 percent reported having another source of health insurance, including COBRA coverage.

As a percentage of the retiree population, about 17 percent reported having family coverage through their own employer and a roughly equal percentage reported having family coverage through their spouse's employer (although officers were much less likely to report the latter).

Obviously, the numbers reported here have some overlap—enrollees may choose to enroll in a variety of different plans. Figure 5.1 shows the percentage of military retirees who had no other health coverage apart from TRICARE or the VA. The figure also shows the percentage of retirees enrolled in one or more civilian health care plans. About 37 percent of officers and 34 percent of enlisted personnel were enrolled in at least one civilian health insurance plan (apart from TRICARE and VA). A small percentage (4–5 percent) were enrolled in more than one civilian plan.

Figure 5.2 examines health care coverage for families of military retirees. About 7–9 percent of military retirees were single with no dependents. About 54–55 percent of the survey population had no other civilian health insurance coverage for their families, while 37–39 percent had families enrolled in one or more civilian plans (31–32 percent in one civilian plan and 5–7 percent in more than one plan).

We also examined the enrollment status of the survey population—the overall status, regardless of whether they had access to or were eligible for civilian health insurance. Across the population, about 57 (53.1, 61.8) percent of officers and 58 (53.0, 62.8) percent of enlisted were not enrolled in any civilian plan (either for self- or family coverage).

Overall, about 8 percent of the retirees were single with no dependents. Among them, about 80 (67.1, 93.0) percent of officers and 76 (59.5, 92.0) percent of the enlisted were not enrolled in civilian plans. Among retirees with families, about 56 percent of both officers and

Figure 5.2
Percentage of Retired Officers and Enlisted Personnel, by Enrollment in Civilian Health Insurance Plans for Family Coverage for Spouse/Dependents, February–March 2006

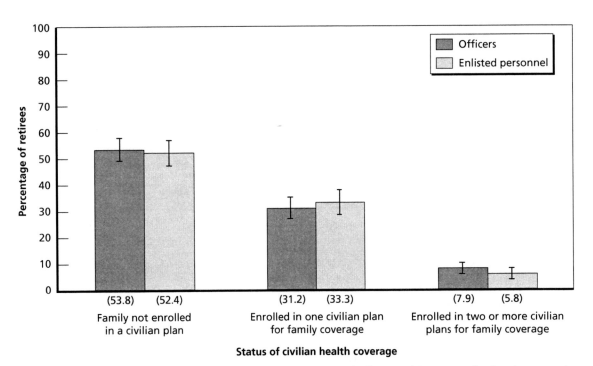

NOTES: The numbers do not add to 100 percent because 7 percent of officers and 9 percent of enlisted personnel were single with no dependents. Confidence intervals are given in Table B.13.
RAND *MG583-5.2*

Figure 5.3
Percentage of Retired Officers and Enlisted Personnel with Families, by Type of Health Insurance Coverage, February–March 2006

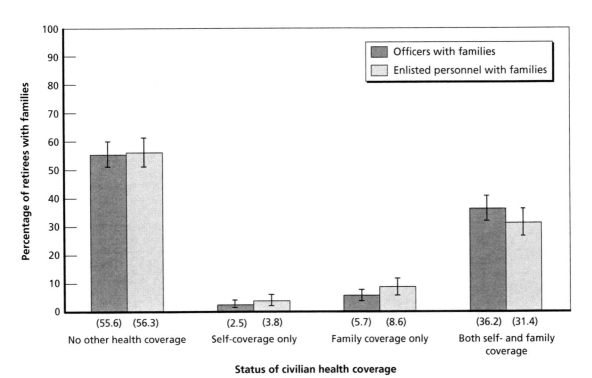

NOTE: Confidence intervals are given in Table B.14.
RAND *MG583-5.3*

enlisted with families were not enrolled in any other type of health plan other than TRICARE or the VA (Figure 5.3). About 2 percent of officers and 4 percent of enlisted personnel had self-coverage only, while 6 percent of officers and 9 percent of enlisted had only family coverage. About 36 percent of officers and 31 percent of enlisted with families had both self- and family coverage.

Reasons for Not Enrolling in Civilian Plan for Which Retirees or Families Were Eligible

As discussed above, many retirees chose not to participate in health insurance plans for which they were eligible, either through their own or their spouse's employer or through a professional association. As shown in Table 5.2, 73 percent of officers and 79 percent of enlisted personnel were eligible to enroll themselves or their families in one or more of these plans. However, 49 percent of eligible officers and 51 percent of eligible enlisted personnel chose not to enroll either themselves or their families in civilian health insurance plans for which they were eligible.

Table 5.2
Percentage of Retired Officers and Enlisted Personnel Eligible to Enroll and Those Currently Not Enrolled in Civilian Plan, February–March 2006

	Officers	Enlisted Personnel	Total Survey Population
	Estimate 95% confidence intervals (lower bound, upper bound)		
Retiree or family eligible to enroll in a civilian plan through an employer or professional association	72.9 (69.0, 76.8)	79.2 (75.2, 83.2)	77.7 (74.5, 80.9)
Of those eligible			
Retiree or family eligible to enroll but not currently enrolled in a civilian plan through an employer or professional association	48.7 (43.7, 53.7)	50.9 (45.3, 56.4)	50.4 (45.9, 54.8)

We asked retirees who were eligible to enroll themselves or their families but chose not to do so the reasons for their nonparticipation. The results are shown in Figure 5.4, which ranks the reasons based on frequency of mention. Because there is little difference in the responses of officers and enlisted personnel, we show only the overall responses. The percentages shown are for those who were eligible to enroll but are not currently enrolled, not for the overall population.

The cost of the premiums is by far the most important reason for not enrolling—mentioned by close to four-fifths of the group—followed by high copays and high deductibles (mentioned by 57–58 percent). About half of the group reported that they preferred doctors in MTFs or TRICARE, and about 30 percent said the lack of choice with respect to doctors or hospitals was a factor in not enrolling. About one-fifth mentioned that the civilian plan did not cover care they thought they needed, while one-tenth complained about the paperwork and reimbursement delays. A very small percentage (5 percent) reported that their employer had provided an incentive to use the military coverage.

We were interested in probing whether the retirees or family members who were not currently enrolled in a civilian plan had ever been enrolled since the retiree left active duty. About 43 (38.0, 47.1) percent of these retirees reported that they or their families had been previously enrolled in a health insurance plan. Of these, about 29 (22.2, 35.9) percent had been enrolled in a plan one to two years prior, and 26 (18.8, 32.1) percent had been enrolled three to four years prior. About 13 (7.7, 18.1) percent reported having been enrolled in a plan more than ten years prior.

Asked why the retiree and/or his or her family decided to discontinue participation in the plan, cost of the plan again surfaced as the most important reason, followed closely by a job change that eliminated access to the plan, mentioned by 48 and 45 percent of the population (see Figure 5.5). About one-fifth reported that the plan was no longer offered. Dissatisfaction with the plan—either in terms of medical care, denial of care, or paperwork—was mentioned by 9–10 percent. Once again, very few mentioned employer-provided incentives to use military coverage as a reason for not continuing their enrollment.

Figure 5.4
Percentage of Military Retirees Not Enrolled in Civilian Health Insurance Plans for Which They or Family Members Are Eligible, by Reason for Non-enrollment, February–March 2006

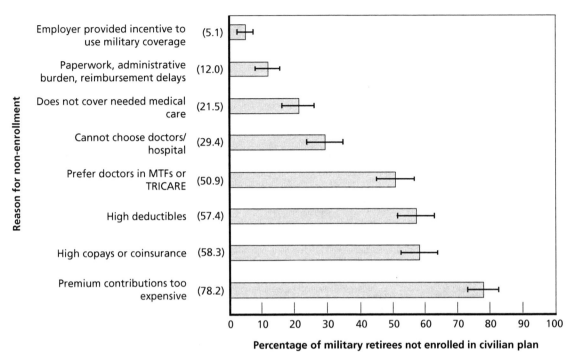

NOTES: An employer's incentives to use military coverage include both those that are and are not specific to TRICARE eligible employees. Confidence intervals are given in Table B.15.
RAND *MG583-5.4*

Current Enrollment in Civilian Health Insurance Plans

As mentioned previously, about 42 percent of the survey population of military retirees was currently enrolled in one or more civilian health care plans. We asked about the reasons why the retiree and/or his or her family chose to enroll in such a plan; respondents provided a yes or no answer for each reason. Figure 5.6 lists these responses. More than half of those currently enrolled mentioned that they preferred the network of doctors/hospitals in the civilian plan, while 49 percent reported that MTFs were not conveniently located as the reasons for enrolling in the civilian plan. About 30 percent were eligible for free coverage through their employer or other non-TRICARE source. About one-quarter reported lack of TRICARE coverage for needed medical care and administrative burden and reimbursement delays associated with TRICARE as reasons for enrollment in a civilian plan. About 20 percent said that their civilian coverage was less costly than TRICARE, and of this group, about half mentioned that the premiums were lower, as were the deductibles and copays. This is in contrast to the earlier results, in which the cost of civilian health insurance was cited as a major deterrent to enrollment. Close to half of the group that mentioned the low cost of civilian health insurance was

Figure 5.5
Percentage of Military Retirees Previously Enrolled in Civilian Health Insurance Plans, by Reason for Discontinuing Enrollment, February–March 2006

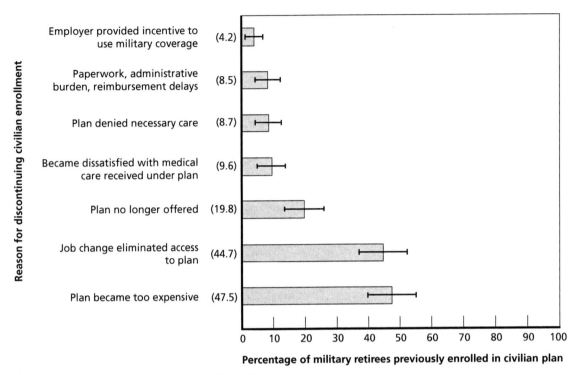

NOTE: Confidence intervals are given in Table B.16.
RAND *MG583-5.5*

employed by the private sector, about one-third paid no premiums for coverage, and another 30 percent paid under $1,000 for their health insurance plan.

Annual Cost of Civilian Health Insurance Premiums

The 2005 KFF/HRET survey results indicated that the average annual premium for covered workers across all plan types was $4,024 for single coverage and $10,880 for family coverage in 2005 (Kaiser Family Foundation and Health Research and Educational Trust, 2005). The cost of the plan varied significantly by type of plan (i.e., conventional, HMO, PPO, point-of-service [POS]). The average employee cost was $610 for single coverage and $2,713 for family coverage, with the remainder being paid by the employer.

We asked retirees about the premiums they paid for their civilian health insurance plans.[2] Table 5.3 shows the annual cost of health insurance plans in which retired officers and

---

[2] Following common practice, we did not ask those who were eligible but not enrolled about the premium contribution they would have paid had they chosen to enroll. It is unlikely that they would be able to reliably report on such amounts

Figure 5.6
Percentage of Military Retirees Currently Enrolled in Civilian Health Insurance Plans, by Reason for Enrollment, February–March 2006

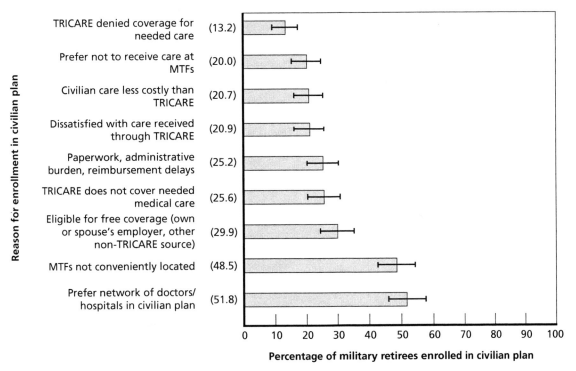

NOTE: Confidence intervals are given in Table B.17.
RAND MG583-5.6

enlisted personnel participated. About 21 percent of officers and 23 percent of enlisted reported that they did not pay any premiums for the plans in which they were enrolled. Officers were more likely to be paying higher annual costs for health insurance, but it is difficult to compare these costs without having more information on the types of benefits offered by the plans and amounts of deductibles and copays. About 16 (10.9, 21.7) percent of officers and 26 (19.1, 33.2) percent of enlisted personnel reported paying a premium of between $1 and $999 per year for health insurance coverage, while 25 (19.0, 31.1) percent of officers and 23 (16.1, 29.8) percent of enlisted personnel paid $2,500 or more for health insurance.

As expected, the annual costs vary by whether the respondent elected self-coverage only or had family coverage. The average premium for self-coverage only was $691 ($444, $939)—which is relatively similar to that reported by the KFF/HRET survey ($610)—and $1,993

___

when they are not actually incurring the expense. Such information is typically gathered from employers and was outside the scope of this study.

Table 5.3
Percentage of Retired Officers and Enlisted Personnel Enrolled in Civilian Health Insurance Plans, by 2005 Annual Insurance Premium, February–March 2006

Annual Insurance Premium for Civilian Plan	Officers	Enlisted Personnel	Total Population
		Estimate 95% confidence intervals (lower bound, upper bound)	
$0	21.4 (15.8, 27.0)	23.3 (16.5, 30.1)	22.8 (17.5, 28.2)
$1–499	7.2 (3.9, 10.4)	9.3 (4.8, 13.7)	8.8 (5.3, 12.3)
$500–999	9.0 (4.6, 13.5)	16.9 (10.8, 23.0)	15.0 (10.3, 19.7)
$1,000–1,499	15.2 (10.2, 20.2)	12.0 (6.9, 17.1)	12.8 (8.7, 16.8)
$1,500–1,999	11.3 (6.3, 16.3)	8.7 (4.3, 13.0)	9.3 (5.8, 12.8)
$2,000–2,499	10.8 (6.7, 15.0)	6.9 (2.9, 11.0)	7.9 (4.7, 11.1)
$2,500–3,499	10.0 (5.8, 14.2)	10.4 (5.4, 15.4)	10.3 (6.4, 14.2)
$3,500 and above	15.1 (10.1, 20.1)	12.5 (7.1, 18.0)	13.1 (8.8, 17.5)

($1,736, $2,249) for both self- and family coverage.[3] The average premium for family coverage was lower than that reported in the KFF/HRET survey in 2004. This is not entirely surprising. Those retirees have access to TRICARE coverage at very favorable rates, so they are unlikely to purchase other health insurance, especially if it is expensive.

Out-of-Pocket Costs

Increasing the amount that people pay directly out of pocket for their health care should encourage people to use less care. Generally, out-of-pocket costs refer to payment for services (such as copays or deductibles), not premiums; we follow this convention here. Overall, the 2003 Medical Expenditure Panel Survey found that people generally paid 20 percent of total health care costs and insurance; other sources picked up the remaining 80 percent, although this percentage varied considerably by level of spending, type of service, and poverty level (Kaiser Family Foundation, 2006).

---

[3] If we include only those paying nonzero premiums, we find that the average premium across the retirees was $1,166 ($803, $1,528) for self-coverage only and $2,344 ($2,072, $2,613) for both self- and family coverage.

Table 5.4 presents estimates of out-of-pocket costs—excluding premiums—among military retirees in the survey population. We find that 15 percent of officers and 20 percent of enlisted reported no out-of-pocket costs in 2005, and another 36–37 percent reported spending less than $500. Thus, median spending was a little less than $500. About 15 percent of officers and 12 percent of enlisted reported spending $2,000 or more out of pocket for medical care, while 7–8 percent reported spending $3,000 or more.

As described in Chapter One, TRICARE Standard has no premium component, but features higher deductibles and copays when coverage is obtained at a civilian facility, and, when MTF space is limited, Prime enrollees are given priority over those with Standard. Prime enrollees, while subject to an annual premium, incur very low copayments for treatment in a civilian network facility. For example, the civilian inpatient cost share for Prime enrollees is $11 per day (or $25 per admission) as compared to as much as $250 per day under TRICARE Extra. When Extra and Standard are second payers to other insurance (i.e., a civilian non-TRICARE plan), only the deductible is assessed in most cases. TRICARE pays up to what it would have paid if it were the only insurer, so it usually picks up costs beyond the deductible. Thus, choosing TRICARE Standard/Extra as primary medical coverage over enrolling in TRICARE Prime or a civilian non-TRICARE plan provides lower up-front costs but runs the risk of higher out-of-pocket costs if significant care outside an MTF is required. This risk is reflected in our survey data. Of those enrolled in either TRICARE Prime or through a civilian non-TRICARE plan, 5.5 (3.5, 7.6) percent incurred high out-of-pocket costs ($3,000 or more), while 14.8 (8.5, 21.2) percent of those relying on TRICARE Standard/Extra

Table 5.4
Percentage of Retired Officers and Enlisted Personnel, by Out-of-Pocket Costs in 2005, February–March 2006

Annual Out-of-Pocket Costs	Officers	Enlisted Personnel	Total Population
	Estimate 95% confidence intervals (lower bound, upper bound)		
$0	14.7 (11.4, 18.0)	20.0 (16.1, 23.9)	18.8 (15.7, 21.9)
$1–499	36.9 (32.5, 41.2)	36.2 (31.4, 41.0)	36.3 (32.5, 40.2)
$500–1,999	33.6 (29.2, 37.9)	32.1 (27.4, 36.8)	32.4 (28.7, 36.1)
$2,000–2,999	7.1 (4.9, 9.3)	4.0 (2.1, 6.0)	4.8 (3.2, 6.3)
$3,000–4,999	5.4 (3.4, 7.4)	5.0 (2.8, 7.1)	5.1 (3.4, 6.8)
$5,000 and above	2.4 (1.1, 3.8)	2.7 (1.0, 4.4)	2.6 (1.3, 4.0)

as their primary coverage had high out-of-pocket expenses, a statistically significant difference (p = 0.01). Of those survey respondents with high out-of-pocket costs (over $3,000), all but one indicated that they or a family member received treatment in a civilian facility.

Price Elasticity of Health Plan Enrollment

Civilian health insurance premiums have risen sharply over the last few years. The 2004 KFF/HRET survey report pointed out that in 2005, "The cost of health insurance rose 9.2% in 2005, less than the 11.2% increase in 2004, but much higher than the overall rate of inflation of 3.5% and the increase in workers' earnings of 2.7%" (Kaiser Family Foundation and Health Research and Educational Trust, 2005, p. 16). Since 2000, the cost of job-based health insurance has rise by 73 percent. Overall, the percentage of the premium paid by workers for single coverage has remained steady at 16 percent, and for family coverage, at 26–28 percent over the last four years; but combined with the increase in total premiums, this has resulted in an increase in the average monthly worker contribution for single and family health insurance. In addition, a recent report by the Robert Wood Johnson Foundation, released in May 2006, reported that although the percentage of the premium paid by the employee has remained stable for the nation as a whole, six states actually saw an increase of 5 percent or more from 1998 to 2003 (State Health Access Data Assistance Center and the Urban Institute, 2006). Twenty-five states experienced a significant decline in the "take-up" rate of employees eligible for health insurance in the private sector (i.e., the percentage of employees who are eligible and enrolled in health insurance offered by their private-sector employer) of between 5 and 12 percent. The cost of insurance was the most frequently cited reason by uninsured individuals for not enrolling in health insurance plans.

Economists quantify the degree of consumer responsiveness to changes in the price of a good by calculating the *own* price elasticity of demand. The own price elasticity of demand measures the percentage change in quantity demanded resulting from a 1 percent change in the price of the good, holding other things constant. Mathematically, elasticity is calculated as the percent change in quantity demanded divided by percent change in price. The magnitude of an elasticity estimate measures how responsive demand is. If the elasticity estimate is greater than one in absolute value, then demand is very responsive or "elastic"; conversely, if the estimate is less than one in absolute value, then demand is said to be price inelastic. Goods that do not have close substitutes tend to have inelastic demands; typically, we expect the demand for health care services to be relatively inelastic because there are few close substitutes for medical services. However, when individuals have the opportunity to enroll in several similar health insurance plans (such as TRICARE and civilian insurance), the probability of enrollment may be very sensitive to premium price.

In the literature on health plan choice, own price elasticities of demand are typically calculated by evaluating the change in the probability of enrolling in a health plan given a change in out-of-pocket premium price (Strombom, Buchmueller, and Feldstein, 2002; Cutler and Reber, 1998; Royalty and Solomon, 1999; Goldman, Leibowitz, and Robalino, 2004; Atherly, Dowd, and Feldman, 2004). In their review of the civilian literature, Ringel et al.

(2002) found that own price elasticities of demand range from –0.10 to –1.75, suggesting that enrollment is moderately to highly sensitive to premium price. Hosek et al. (1995) used a series of hypothetical questions to calculate the own elasticity of demand with respect to premium price for a DoD population, and they estimated that a 10-percent change in premiums would be associated with a 4.7-percent decline in enrollment for military retirees under the age of 65. While the estimates from Hosek et al. (1995) are informative, they were based on questions designed to assess DoD beneficiaries' interest in HMO-style civilian health care plans over CHAMPUS. Both the DoD health system and the civilian health insurance market have changed significantly since the questionnaire was fielded—with DoD replacing CHAMPUS with TRICARE, and with the civilian market becoming increasingly dominated by PPOs.

In our survey, we asked retirees who were enrolled in a civilian health plan whether they would give up this coverage and increase reliance on TRICARE if their civilian premiums rose by 25 percent above the current amount. Table 5.5 shows their responses. As we saw earlier, about 42 percent of the survey population was enrolled in one or more civilian health insurance plans. Of these, about half reported that they would give up their civilian plan if the premiums rose by 25 percent. This decision did not appear to be related to the current premium amount. This evidence is suggestive because it is based on hypothetical questions; to fully evaluate elasticities, we would need to observe the choices that retirees make given an actual change in premium price.

Nevertheless, we can use these numbers to calculate a rough estimate of the own price elasticity of demand. Civilian health plan enrollment, according to our estimate, is very elastic, –2.0 with respect to premiums; that is, if premiums increase by 10 percent, enrollment may decline by 20 percent. Although this figure is slightly larger than the elasticities reported above, DoD retirees might be particularly responsive to increases in civilian premiums due to their high familiarity with and access to the TRICARE system. Previous research argues that demand is less elastic when enrollees are less familiar with outside health insurance options (Buchmueller and Feldstein, 1997). Our survey revealed that almost 70 percent of retirees enrolled in civilian coverage also used TRICARE in 2005, suggesting a high degree of reliance on TRICARE. Our results further suggest that between 14 and 16 percent of DoD retirees

Table 5.5
Percentage of Retired Officers and Enlisted Personnel Currently Enrolled in Civilian Plan, by Reported Change in Behavior, if Premiums for Civilian Plan Rose by 25 Percent, February–March 2006

	Officers	Enlisted Personnel	Total Population
	Estimate 95% confidence intervals (lower bound, upper bound)		
Retiree and/or family member enrolled in civilian plan	42.6 (38.2, 46.9)	42.1 (37.2, 47.0)	42.2 (38.3, 46.1)
Of those enrolled and paying a premium			
Would give up civilian plan if premiums for civilian plan rose by 25%	48.3 (40.0, 56.6)	52.1 (43.1, 61.1)	51.3 (44.1, 58.5)
Of population			
Would give up civilian plan if premiums for civilian plan rose by 25%	13.7 (10.7, 16.7)	16.4 (12.7, 20.1)	15.8 (12.9, 18.7)

would drop their current coverage and presumably depend entirely on TRICARE and/or VA coverage if civilian premiums rose by 25 percent. Obviously, this is only a rough approximation—we know that there is a considerable chasm between intentions and behavior. What is important is that retirees appear to be quite conscious of price—and large price increases for civilian health insurance may result in a substantial shift to TRICARE usage.

Military retirees who were eligible for civilian health insurance but had not enrolled in such plans were asked whether they would enroll in these plans if civilian premiums were to decline by 25 percent from their current level. Their responses are shown in Table 5.6. As we had shown earlier, about 73 percent of officers and 79 percent of enlisted were eligible for civilian health insurance, either through their own or their spouse's employer or through a professional association or union. Between 49 and 51 percent of those eligible had chosen not to take advantage of such access. Of this group, very few—less than 10 percent of officers and 21 percent of enlisted—reported that they would enroll in the civilian plan for which they were eligible if premiums fell by 25 percent, giving us an own price elasticity of demand of −0.38 for officers, −0.86 for enlisted personnel, and −0.76 overall. These elasticity estimates are within the range of estimates reported in the prior literature (see Ringel et al., 2002). Of the population as whole, only about 3 percent of officers and 9 percent of enlisted would enroll in a civilian plan if prices fell.

The sharp difference in the responses to questions about *increases* versus *decreases* in civilian-plan premiums likely reflect a difference between those currently enrolled in civilian plans and those who have chosen not to enroll in these plans. Most retirees who are enrolled are paying a premium contribution, and their preference for civilian insurance does not appear to be strong enough to prevent their dropping the insurance if the premium *increases*. In contrast, retirees who have not enrolled in a civilian plan are probably avoiding a substantial premium contribution and would not reconsider their decision even if the civilian premiums were to substantially *decrease*.

We emphasize that these elasticities are very rough; not only are they based on hypothetical questions, they also focus on a single discrete change in price. In theory, elasticities are meant to measure the impact of an inframarginal change in price on quantity purchased. Many previous studies that estimated the price elasticity of health plan choice exploited policy changes that led to discrete increases in out-of-pocket premiums (Strombom, Buchmueller, and Feldstein, 2002; Cutler and Reber, 1998; Royalty and Solomon, 1999; Goldman, Leibowitz, and Robalino, 2004), although—since premium changes are typically phased-in over several years—these studies often observed variation in price and enrollment across several discrete intervals. In our case, we ask about only one relatively large (25 percent) change in premium price. It is possible that our elasticity estimates would be different had we asked about a 5- percent or 50-percent change. Finally, our survey questionnaire did not specify whether other attributes of the insurance contract (e.g., deductibles and copayments) would remain fixed under the hypothetical premium change. If respondents assumed that an increase in civilian premiums would be accompanied by a change in the insurance contract, then our elasticity estimates will be biased downward. Yet, despite the many caveats surrounding our elasticity estimates, we report them because they align reasonably well with estimates in the published literature. They also are suggestive of a potential "stickiness" in

TRICARE reliance: Those who are currently enrolled in civilian health insurance appear quite willing to switch to TRICARE if their premiums increase. In contrast, TRICARE users who are eligible for civilian health insurance but not enrolled appear unlikely to increase their reliance on the civilian sector—even if civilian premiums fall relative to TRICARE.

Table 5.6
Percentage of Retired Officers and Enlisted Personnel Eligible for but Not Currently Enrolled in Civilian Plan, by Reported Change in Behavior if Premiums for Civilian Plan Fell by 25 Percent, February–March 2006

	Officers	Enlisted Personnel	Total Population
	Estimate 95% confidence intervals (lower bound, upper bound)		
Retiree or family eligible to enroll in a civilian plan through an employer or professional association	72.9 (69.0, 76.8)	79.2 (75.2, 83.2)	77.7 (74.5, 80.9)
Of those eligible			
Retiree or family eligible to enroll but not currently enrolled in a civilian plan through an employer or professional association	48.7 (43.7, 53.7)	50.9 (45.3, 56.4)	50.4 (45.9, 54.8)
Of those not currently enrolled			
Would enroll in civilian plan for which they are currently eligible if premiums for civilian plan fell by 25%	9.5 (5.4, 13.7)	21.4 (15.3, 27.5)	19.1 (14.1, 24.1)
Of population			
Would enroll in civilian plan for which they are currently eligible if premiums for civilian plan fell by 25%	3.2 (1.8, 4.7)	9.2 (6.4, 12.0)	7.8 (5.6, 9.9)

Use of TRICARE for Medical Care and Prescription Costs

This chapter examines the use of TRICARE to cover the costs of medical care and prescription medications, especially among those retirees who had obtained civilian health insurance.

Usage and Source of Medical Care

Retirees were asked whether they and their families had received medical care during 2005 and if so, where that care was received—civilian facilities (including doctor's offices or hospitals and facilities run by civilian TRICARE contractors), MTFs, and/or other facilities, such as VA or USFHP clinics). Figure 6.1 shows the locations where military retirees received medical care in 2005, and Figure 6.2 shows the same information for families of military retirees.

A small percentage of retirees—just under 10 percent—reported that they did not receive any medical care in 2005. About 39 percent of enlisted and 45 percent of officers received care at a civilian facility only, and another 12–16 percent chose to go only to a military facility. Few (2 percent of officers and 6 percent of enlisted) received care at a VA or USFHP facility only. Some received care at two types of facilities—the most common being a civilian facility and an MTF (15–18 percent). We see a similar pattern among families of military retirees. A small percentage did not have spouses or dependents, and a few reported that their families did not receive medical care in 2005. Most received care at a civilian facility only (47–52 percent) or at a civilian facility and an MTF (18–21 percent).

Retirees were also asked how they paid for such care, that is, what health insurance coverage they relied on for this care—TRICARE, non-TRICARE civilian plan, or VA coverage. We disaggregated the responses by whether retirees had enrolled in a civilian plan or not, where enrollment included self-coverage only, family coverage only, or both self- and family coverage. Figures 6.3 and 6.4 show the responses for officers and enlisted personnel, respectively. The categories shown are mutually exclusive.

Not surprisingly, among officers who were not enrolled in a civilian plan, over 90 percent reported that they relied on TRICARE or a combination of TRICARE and VA for medical care. A small group, however, reported that they used a non-TRICARE civilian plan to

Figure 6.1
Percentage of Retired Officers and Enlisted Personnel, by Type of Facility Where They Received Medical Care in 2005, February–March 2006

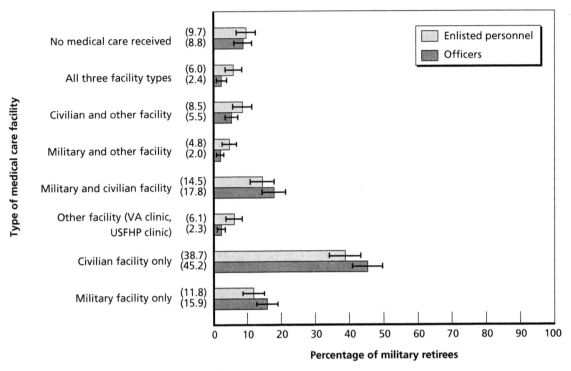

NOTE: Confidence intervals are given in Table B.18.

RAND *MG583-6.1*

pay for medical care.[1] Those who were enrolled in a non-TRICARE civilian plan relied on a mix of both TRICARE and non-TRICARE civilian plans for health insurance. For example, 38 percent said that they relied exclusively on the non-TRICARE civilian plan, while 36 percent said they relied on both TRICARE and the non-TRICARE plan. Eight percent said that they relied on TRICARE exclusively. The annual cost of the non-TRICARE civilian plan was a statistically significant predictor ($p = 0.018$) of exclusive reliance on TRICARE, with the probability of exclusive reliance on TRICARE dropping significantly as premium costs for the non-TRICARE civilian plan increased. For example, when the non-TRICARE premium was $1,000, the estimated probability of exclusive reliance on TRICARE was a low 0.06; when the premium increased to $3,000, that estimate dropped by another two-thirds—to 0.02. Overall, 53 percent of officers reported that they relied on TRICARE for all or some of their medical care.

---

[1] Possible explanations for this discrepancy include the following: the survey did not fully capture all possible non-TRICARE civilian sources of health insurance (including sources that do not require enrollment); respondents included other civilian sources of medical coverage when answering, such as workers' compensation or automobile medical payments; or respondents found the item confusing.

Figure 6.2
Percentage of Families of Military Retirees, by Type of Facility Where They Received Medical Care in 2005, February–March 2006

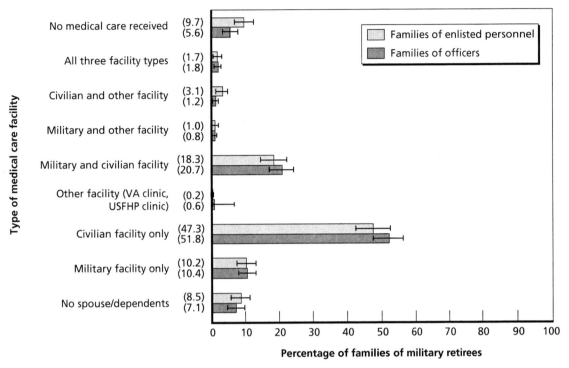

NOTE: Confidence intervals are given in Table B.19.
RAND *MG583-6.2*

Among enlisted personnel who were enrolled in a non-TRICARE civilian plan, we see much the same pattern of using a mix of TRICARE and non-TRICARE civilian sources of health insurance with an interesting exception: Enlisted personnel were much more likely to report using VA coverage. For example, 21 percent of enlisted personnel reported using VA for medical care (in combination with TRICARE and a civilian plan), compared with 8 percent of officers. Enlisted personnel not enrolled in anything other than TRICARE also showed a greater usage of VA coverage than did officers. While the differences noted here were not statistically significant, the individual usage estimates offer useful information about patterns of usage among officers and enlisted personnel. Overall, among all retirees enrolled in a civilian plan, 51 (44.8, 56.7) percent reported using their TRICARE coverage.

Figure 6.3
Percentage of Retired Officers, by Enrollment in Civilian Plan and Type of Health Insurance Coverage Used for Medical Care in 2005, February–March 2006

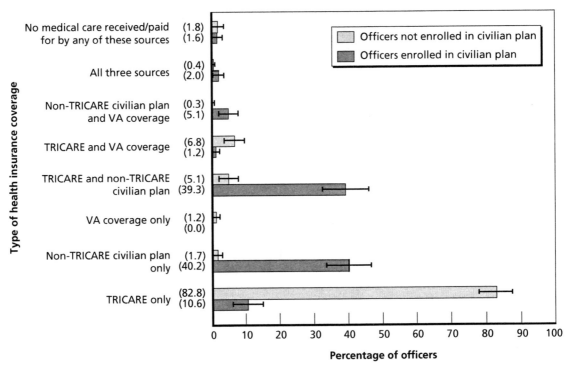

NOTE: Confidence intervals are given in Table B.20.
RAND *MG583-6.3*

Coverage for Prescriptions

We are primarily interested in the extent to which individuals and families who are enrolled in non-TRICARE civilian plans use TRICARE. Here, we examine usage of health insurance to pay for prescriptions among the group that was enrolled in one or more of these plans. Figure 6.5 reports the percentage of officers and enlisted personnel who relied on non-TRICARE civilian health insurance, TRICARE, and VA coverage to pay for prescription drugs.

Many military retirees enrolled in a non-TRICARE civilian plan used TRICARE for coverage of prescription drugs. For example, while only 40 percent of officers and 30 percent of enlisted personnel reported using only the non-TRICARE plan for prescription drugs, a much larger percentage relied on TRICARE (either exclusively or in conjunction with other coverage). For example, 19 percent of both officers and enlisted personnel relied on TRICARE exclusively, another 30–34 percent relied on both TRICARE and non-TRICARE plans, 2–3 percent relied only on TRICARE and VA coverage, and 2–5 percent relied on all three sources. Thus, 57 percent of retirees enrolled in a non-TRICARE civilian plan reported relying on TRICARE to some extent for their prescription drug coverage. Enlisted personnel again

Figure 6.4
Percentage of Retired Enlisted Personnel, by Enrollment in Civilian Plan and Type of Health Insurance Coverage Used for Medical Care in 2005, February–March 2006

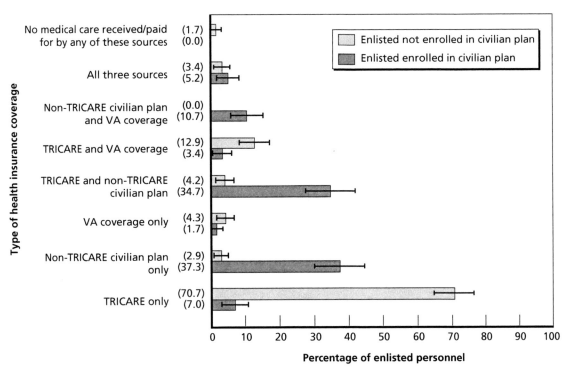

NOTE: Confidence intervals are given in Table B.20.

RAND *MG583-6.4*

appeared to take advantage of their VA coverage to a greater extent than did officers, although largely in combination with one of the other two plans.

Figure 6.5
Percentage of Retired Officers and Enlisted Personnel Enrolled in Civilian Plan, by Type of Health Insurance Coverage Used to Cover Prescriptions in 2005, February–March 2006

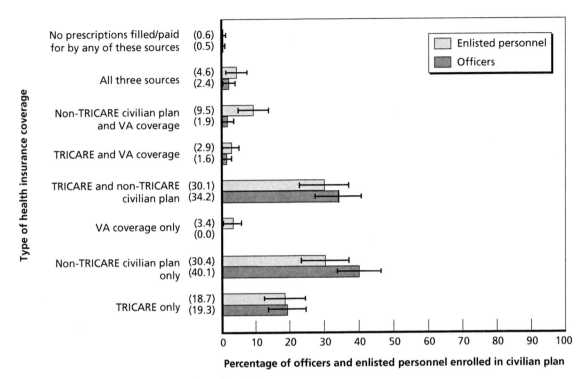

NOTE: Confidence intervals are given in Table B.21.

RAND *MG583-6.5*

CHAPTER SEVEN

Conclusions

This study attempted to measure military retirees' access to and participation in civilian health insurance plans, other than TRICARE, through a pilot, computer-assisted telephone survey with responses from more than 900 retired officers and enlisted personnel. The survey population consisted of all officers and enlisted personnel under age 65 who were living in CONUS, and who had been retired for at least one year (i.e., retired on or before June 30, 2004). We received a 60-percent response rate on the survey.

Findings

A Large Number of Retirees Have Access to Civilian Health Insurance

Overall, about 80 percent of the survey population was employed—78 percent of officers and 81 percent of enlisted personnel. About 87 percent of retirees ages 60 years or younger were employed, compared with 53 percent of those between 61 and 64 years. Well over four-fifths of the military retirees were currently married and living with their spouses. About 54 percent of spouses of officers and 62 percent of spouses of enlisted personnel were employed.

Overall, about 75 percent of the survey population had access to another source of health insurance, and about 77 percent of those with families had access to family coverage. If we count all sources of coverage for either the retirees or their families, we find that 78 percent of the survey population reported having access to some other form of health insurance for themselves and/or their families through their own or their spouse's employer or a professional association. Overall, about 73 percent of officers and 79 percent of enlisted personnel were eligible to enroll themselves or their families in their own or their spouse's employer-provided plans or through plans offered by professional associations or unions (Table 7.1).

A Substantial Percentage Chose Not to Enroll, Citing Cost of Premiums

About half of those who were eligible chose not to enroll either themselves or their families in civilian health insurance plans for which they were eligible (see Table 7.1). Overall, 39 percent of the population was enrolled in an employer-provided civilian plan or through a professional association. Retirees and their families had other sources of health insurance—directly purchased from insurance companies or, perhaps, COBRA coverage. Adding enroll-

Table 7.1
Percentage of Retired Officers and Enlisted Personnel Eligible to Enroll and Those Currently Enrolled in Civilian Plans, February–March 2006

Those Eligible to Enroll	Officers	Enlisted Personnel	Total Population
Retiree or family eligible to enroll in a civilian plan through an employer or professional association	72.9 (69.0, 76.8)	79.2 (75.2, 83.2)	77.7 (74.5, 80.9)
Retiree or family eligible to enroll *but not currently enrolled* in a civilian plan through an employer or professional association	35.5 (31.6, 39.5)	40.3 (35.4, 45.1)	39.1 (35.4, 42.9)
Retiree or family eligible to enroll *and currently enrolled* in a civilian plan through an employer or professional association	37.4 (33.1, 41.6)	38.9 (34.1, 43.7)	38.5 (34.7, 42.3)
Total percent enrolled in civilian plan (self and/or family) offered by employers, professional associations, insurance companies, and other sources	42.6 (38.2, 46.9)	42.1 (37.2, 47.0)	42.2 (38.3, 46.1)

NOTE: *Eligible to enroll* means that at least one family member (retiree, spouse, or dependent) was eligible. *Not currently enrolled* means that no family member was enrolled.

ment through these sources, we find that 42 percent of the survey population was enrolled in a civilian plan and had either self- and/or family coverage.

The cost of the premiums is by far the most important reason for not enrolling—mentioned by close to four-fifths of the group, followed by high copays and high deductibles (mentioned by 56–57 percent). About half of the group reported that they preferred doctors in MTFs or TRICARE, and about 30 percent said the lack of choice with respect to doctors/hospitals was a factor in not enrolling.

Across the population, about 10 percent of military retirees were offered incentives by either their own or their spouse's employers not to enroll in civilian insurance plans, but only about 2 percent reported that such incentives were specific to TRICARE-eligible employees.

Demand for Civilian Employer-Provided Health Insurance Appears Highly Elastic to Price Increases but Inelastic to Price Decreases

About 21 percent of officers and 23 percent of enlisted retirees who were enrolled in a civilian health insurance plan reported that they did not pay any premiums for the plans in which they were enrolled. About 16 percent of officers and 26 percent of enlisted personnel reported paying less than $1,000 per year for health insurance coverage, while 25 percent of officers and 23 percent of enlisted personnel paid $2,500 or more for health insurance. The average premium for self-coverage only was $691, an amount higher than that reported in the KFF/HRET survey, but still within the margin of error.

The cost of medical care was $1,993 for both self- and family coverage. The average premium for family coverage was lower than that reported in the KFF/HRET survey in 2005 ($2,713). This is not entirely surprising, since these retirees have access to TRICARE coverage at very favorable rates; for this reason, they are unlikely to purchase other health insurance, especially if it is expensive. Of the 42 percent enrolled in civilian plans, about half reported that they would give up their civilian plan if the premiums rose by 25 percent. Thus, health plan enrollment, according to our estimate, is very elastic: –2.0 with respect to premiums; that is, if premiums increase by 10 percent, enrollment may decline by 20 percent.

About half of the military retirees who were eligible for health insurance had not enrolled in such plans. Asked whether they would enroll in these plans if premiums were to decline by 25 percent from their current level, very few—less than 10 percent of officers and 21 percent of enlisted—reported that they would enroll in the civilian plan for which they were eligible if premiums fell by 25 percent, giving us a demand elasticity of –0.38 for officers, –0.86 for enlisted personnel, and –0.76 overall. Of the population as whole, only about 3 percent of officers and 9 percent of enlisted personnel would enroll in a plan if prices fell.

As we had noted, the marked difference in the responses to questions about *increases* versus *decreases* in the cost of civilian-plan premiums likely reflects a difference between those currently enrolled in civilian plans and those who have chosen not to enroll in those plans. The responses appear to suggest that the preference of retirees enrolled in civilian plans is not strong enough to compensate for price increases—thus, many would drop the insurance if they were faced with a large increase in premiums. In contrast, retirees who have not enrolled in a civilian plan are probably avoiding a high premium contribution and would not reconsider their decision, even if the premiums were to substantially *decrease*.

Those Enrolled in Non-TRICARE Civilian Plans Continue to Rely on TRICARE for Medical Care and Prescription Drug Coverage

Thirty-nine percent of enlisted and 45 percent of officers received care at a civilian facility only and another 12–16 percent chose to go to a military facility only. Few (2 percent of officers and 6 percent of enlisted personnel) received care at a VA or USFHP facility only. Some received care at two types of facilities—the most common being a civilian facility and an MTF (15–18 percent). We see a similar pattern among families of military retirees.

Those who were enrolled in a non-TRICARE civilian plan relied on a mix of both TRICARE and non-TRICARE civilian plans for health insurance, despite being enrolled in civilian plans. For example, only 38 percent of this group said they relied exclusively on the non-TRICARE civilian plan. A similar percentage said they relied on both TRICARE and the non-TRICARE plan, while 8 percent said they relied on TRICARE exclusively. We see much the same pattern among enlisted personnel who were enrolled in a non-TRICARE civilian plan, although enlisted personnel were much more likely to report using VA coverage. Overall, 51 percent of those enrolled in a non-TRICARE civilian plan reported that they relied on TRICARE for all or some of their medical care.

Military retirees enrolled in a non-TRICARE civilian plan also relied heavily on TRICARE for coverage of prescription drugs. For example, while only 40 percent of officers and 30 percent of enlisted personnel reported using only the non-TRICARE plan for prescription drugs, a much larger percentage relied on TRICARE (either exclusively or in conjunction with other coverage). Overall, 56 percent of retirees enrolled in a non-TRICARE civilian plan reported relying on TRICARE to some extent for their prescription drug coverage.

Policy Implications

DoD's FY2007 budget request proposed raising TRICARE enrollment fees, deductibles, and pharmacy copays for retirees to decrease the difference between cost sharing in TRICARE and civilian plans. However, Congress did not support these changes; the final authorization bill rules out any changes through the end of calendar year 2007. The DoD hopes that narrowing the premium contribution gap could lead to a shift *away* from TRICARE, or at least discourage further shifts *to* TRICARE.

While, undoubtedly, price increases will lead to some decrease in the quantity demanded of medical care, it is not clear how large the cost savings would be. The savings would depend on several factors—among other things, the relative rate of increase in civilian and TRICARE health insurance premiums and trends in accessibility to such plans in the civilian sector (given that some small firms are opting *not* to offer health insurance in the face of rising costs). In any case, as long as DoD premiums are considerably lower than civilian premiums, small increases in TRICARE premiums are unlikely to result in noticeable shifts away from TRICARE usage. Further, if TRICARE premiums remain stable while premiums in the civilian sector escalate, TRICARE usage is likely to increase. Data from annual Kaiser Family Foundation and Health Research Educational Trust Survey (2005) indicate that civilian premium contributions for family insurance coverage increased by 46 percent between 1996 and 2005. Our findings show that while a substantial majority of the retiree population is eligible for civilian health insurance, about half of those eligible choose not to enroll, primarily for cost reasons. Those who are enrolled appear to (1) be highly responsive to increases in the cost of civilian health insurance and would likely drop such coverage if costs rose substantially and (2) continue to rely on TRICARE for some of their medical care even if they enroll in a civilian plan.

The results from the survey offer useful information on retirees' health care status, enrollment in civilian health care plans, usage of TRICARE, and sensitivity to changes in the price of civilian plans. Such information, combined with other data, can be used to analyze the effects of TRICARE benefit design changes. Follow-on work at RAND is using these survey results, combined with other data, to assess usage of TRICARE medical care and military facilities and the implications of benefit design changes on health care utilization and expenditures.

However, the survey we fielded, while providing important information, was a pilot study with a small sample size. Understanding the potential impact of an increase in TRICARE premiums will require more complete information than we collected. For example, to fully model the impact of a premium increase for TRICARE, we need data on the civilian premium amounts faced by those who did not enroll, reasons for choosing to enroll in TRICARE Prime, and better precision on the estimates of interest than was possible with our limited sample size. Civilian employers may be considering multiple options for keeping their own expenditures for health care lower, including raising employee contribution amounts or considering plans with higher employee deductibles and copayments. Since most respondents did not know the premium contributions, deductibles, and copayments required for health plans in which they were not enrolled, this information would need to be collected from employers rather than individuals. In addition, the survey would need to ask directly about the impact of proposed changes in

TRICARE fees and copays and likely future changes in civilian health plans on the use of both civilian and TRICARE medical care. A more complete understanding of choices and likely behavior in the face of increasing premiums and copays for TRICARE would require a larger survey that collected data from both retirees and their civilian employers.

Survey of Military Retirees, 2005

The 2005 Survey of Military Retirees was administered as a Computer Assisted Telephone Interview (CATI). The version below served as a template for the CATI computer program used during the actual administration. The protocol began with an introduction to the survey.

Notes inserted that appear in all capital letters were designed for the CATI programmer, to assist in properly tracking the skip patterns and item phrasing.

When two or more choices appear in brackets separated by a slash, e.g., "[you/you and your family/your family members]," the correct choice, based on the respondent's prior answers, is read by the interviewer. The correct choice is tracked within the CATI program and automatically prompted to the interviewer.

When a phrase is enclosed in braces, e.g., "{and your family}," it is read by the interviewer only if appropriate, based on the respondent's prior answers. The correct phrasing is also tracked within the CATI program and automatically prompted to the interviewer.

Notes framed in boxes are questions and answers (Q&A) for the interviewer to use in responding to questions; these notes are also integrated into the CATI program.

INTRODUCTION/INFORMED CONSENT

DIAL THE RESPONDENT (NOTED BELOW AS "R"). WHEN A PERSON ANSWERS THE PHONE:

1.   Hello, my name is _____ and I am calling from the RAND Corporation. May I please speak to [Mr./Mrs. LAST NAME]?

        IF R ANSWERS PHONE OR COMES TO PHONE→GO TO 2

        IF R IS NOT AVAILABLE OR NOT HOME →   GO TO 7

2.   Hello, [Mr./Mrs. LAST NAME]. My name is [NAME] and I'm calling from the RAND Corporation regarding a survey of military retirees. We recently sent a letter providing you information about the survey and its purpose but I'd like to repeat some of that information now.

RAND, a non-profit research institution, is conducting a study of health care options available to military retirees. The Department of Defense is sponsoring the study. The goal of the study is to formulate policies to best serve retirees' health care needs.

We are conducting interviews to learn about retiree health care options. We are interested in talking to people who retired from active duty over the past 20 years and are under age 65 We are contacting you because you are part of a scientifically selected sample of such retirees.

RAND will use the information you provide for research purposes only. We will not disclose your identity or information that would identify you to anyone outside of the project without your permission, exept as reqired by law. We will destroy all information that identifies you at the end of the study.

Taking part in this interview is voluntary. Let me know if you don't want to participate or you want to stop at any time. You should feel free to skip any qestions that you prefer not to answer. The interview will take about 15 minutes. The survey is approved by DoD, and we have an approval tracking number. Would you like to have this number for future reference? Note to interviewer: If yes, say "The survey is authoried under Report Control Symbol number DD-HA(OT) 2223 in accordance with DoD 801   -M 'DoD Procedures for Management of Information Requests'. "]

If after the interview you have any qestions or concerns about the study, you may call the principal investigator for the study on our toll-free number. The principal investigator is Dr. Sheila Kby   and she can be reached at 1-8 -22 -9   ek 322 or you can email her at Sheila_Kby@rand.org.

Q: What do you mean "except as reqired by law?"

A: It means that it is possible RAND's research records could get audited, although this has never happened. It also means that it is possible someone would attempt to subpoena the research data, but again RAND has never been forced to turn over identifiable data in response to a subpoena. Please remember that all information that identifies you will be destroyed by May 20.

---

3.   Do you have any qestions or concerns about participating in this study that I can answer for you at this time?

                YES→REFER TO FAQ'S AND ANSWER R'S QESTIONS/CONCERNS

                NO

4   Is this a good time to do the interview?

                IF R REFSES: →   ATTEMPT TO ADDRESS CONCERNS AND CONVRT
                REFSAL   OR SEE IF R WOLD B WILLING TO SCHEDLE   APPOINTMENT FOR

ANOTHER TIME OR TO HAVE SUPERVISOR CALL THEM IF NECESSARY. IF NO, COMPLETE REFUSAL/BREAK-OFF FORM

IF R WANTS TO GET ANOTHER COPY OF LETTER BEFORE PARTICIPATING→GO TO 5

IF R INDICATES THAT IT IS NOT A GOOD TIME: → GO TO 6.

IF YES, SAY:

> That's great. Thank you. Before we get started I just want to let you know that for the purposes of quality control, my supervisor may monitor this call. →START SURVEY.

5   IF R WANTS ANOTHER COPY OF LETTER BEFORE DOING SURVEY:

I would be happy to mail you the letter again if you like. Let me confirm your mailing address. The address I have is [ADDRESS] Is that correct?

> IF YES→Great. I will send you the letter again. →GO TO 5

> IF NO→What is the correct mailing address? [RECORD ADDRESS] Thank you. I will send you the letter again. →GO TO 5

5.   May we go ahead and schedule an appointment to call you back?

> IF YES→ GO TO 6

> IF NO→Okay, thank you. We will call you back in a few days, after you have received the letter.

6.   Is there a day and time that would be more convenient for you?
SCHEDULE CALL BACK APPOINTMENT.

7   When would be a good time to call [Mr./Mrs. LAST NAME] back?

> DON'T KNOW→ SCHEDULE SOFT CALL BACK FOR DIFFERENT DAY/TIME.

> INFORMANT OFFERS DAY/TIME→ SCHEDULE CALL BACK APPOINTMENT.

SURVEY ITEMS

Employment

We would like to start by asking you about your current employment.

1. Are you currently working for pay?

    a. Yes (skip to Q. 3)

    b. No

2. Are you currently not working because of a disability?

    a. Yes (skip to Q. 6)

    b. No (skip to Q. 6)

3. Are you:

    a. A government employee

        • IF YES: Do you work for the:

            a. Federal government

            b. State government

            c. Local government

    b. Self-employed in your own business, professional practice, or farm

    c. A paid employee of a private or public company, business or individual.

    IF MORE THAN ONE ANSWER:

        • What is your primary employment?

        _____

IF MORE THAN ONE EMPLOYER, PLEASE CODE FOLLOW-ON CATEGORY SO THAT ALL EMPLOYERS MENTIONED IN Q3 ARE LISTED.

Q: What do you mean by primary employment?

A: The job that you rely on most heavily in terms of income. If income is the same at both jobs, then the job to which you devote the greatest number of hours.

4. Thinking about your current employment, how many hours do you typically work per week?

    a. Full-time, 35 hours or more

    b. Part-time, 20 hours or more

    c. Part-time, less than 20 hours

5. Thinking about your current employment, counting all locations where this employer operates, what is the total number of persons who work for this employer? IF NECESSARY, SAY: Please give us your best estimate.

    a. 1 – 9

    b. 10 – 24

    c. 25 – 99

    d. 100 – 199

    e. 200-499

    f. 500 – 999

    g. 1000 or more

    h. Don't know/Not sure

Marital Status and Spouse's Employment Status

I'd like to ask you some qestions about your marital status.

6 Are you now:

    a. Married

    b. Living together but not married

    c. Separated

    d. Divorced (skip to Q. 11)

    e. Widowed (skip to Q. 11)

    f. Single, never been married (skip to Q. 11)

IN SUBEQUENT QUESTIONS THAT ASK ABUT [SPOUSE/PARTNER], PLEASE USE THE TERM "SPOUSE" IF MARRIED OR SEPARATED (Q7A OR Q7C) AND USE THE TERM PARTNER IF LIVING TOGETHER BUT NOT MARRIED (Q7B)

7 Is your [spouse/partner] currently working for pay?

    a. Yes

    b. No (skip to Q. 11)

8. Is your [spouse/partner]:

    a. A government employee

        • IF YES: Does your [spouse/partner] work for the:

            a. Federal government

            b. State government

            c. Local government

    b. Self-employed in his or her own business, professional practice, or farm

    c. A paid employee of a private or public company, business, or individual.

IF MORE THAN ONE ANSWER:

- What is your [spouse/partner]'s primary employment?

_____

IF MORE THAN ONE EMPLOYER, PLEASE CODE FOLLOW-ON CATEGORY SO THAT ALL EMPLOYERS MENTIONED IN Q8 ARE LISTED.

SEE Q&A FOR QUESTION 3.

9. Thinking about your [spouse/partner]'s current employment, how many hours does your [spouse/partner] typically work per week?

    a. Full-time, 35 hours or more

    b. Part-time, 20 hours or more

    c. Part-time, less than 20 hours

10. Thinking about your [spouse/partner]'s current employment, counting all locations where this employer operates, what is the total number of persons who work for this employer? IF NECESSARY, SAY: Please give us your best estimate.

    a. 1 - 9

    b. 10 - 24

    c. 25 - 99

    d. 100 – 199

    e. 200-499

    f. 500 – 999

    g. 1000 or more

    h. DON'T KNOW

11. In 2005, before taxes, what was your total household income from work performed at any job including bonuses, overtime, tips and commissions or other compensation such as retirement pay or unemployment? Please include income and other compensation earned by all household members over the age of 15.

    a.   Up to $25,000

    b. $25,001-50,000

    c. $50,001-75,000

    d. $75,001-100,000

    e. $100,001 or more

CREATE A VARIABLE CALLED "MARSTATUS"

MARSTATUS=0 (SINGLE) IF RESPONDENT CHECKED Q6d, e, or f.

MARSTATUS=1 (MARRIED, SPOUSE NOT EMPLOYED) IF RESPONDENT CHECKED Q6a, b, or c AND Q7="NO".

MARSTATUS=2 (MARRIED, SPOUSE EMPLOYED) IF RESPONDENT CHECKED Q6a, b, or c AND Q7="YES".

12. {Not counting your [spouse/partner],} how many dependents do you have? Please only include dependents who are eligible for retiree medical benefits under TRICARE.

    a.   0

    b.   1

    c.   2

    d.   3

    e.   4 or more

> Q: What do you mean by eligible for medical retiree benefits?
>
> A: Generally, all children are eligible until age 21, unless the child is a full-time student (validation of student status required) then eligibility ends at age 23 or when the full-time student status ends, whichever comes first. Children remain eligible even if parents divorce or remarry. Eligibility may extend past age 21 if the child is incapable of self-support because of a mental or physical incapacity and the condition existed prior to age 21, or if the condition occurred between the ages of 21 and 23 while the child was a full-time student.

Provision of and Participation in Non-TRICARE Civilian Employer-Provided Health Insurance

We would now like to ask about non-TRICARE civilian health insurance options available to you and your family. We are interested in whether you have such options available, regardless of whether you are currently enrolled in them or use them. We are talking about health insurance coverage, not about dental or vision plans or life insurance. Please do not include supplemental insurance plans that can only be used to pay for co-pays, deductibles, and other expenses not covered by TRICARE. Now I'd like to ask you about your non-TRICARE civilian health insurance options.

IF Q1="NO" AND MARSTATUS=0, 1, SKIP TO Q. 19

IF Q1="NO" AND MARSTATUS=2, SKIP TO Q. 16

13. Are you currently eligible to enroll in a health insurance plan offered by your employer?

   a. Yes

   b. No (IF MARSTATUS=0, 1, skip to Q. 19, IF MARSTATUS=2, SKIP TO Q16)

> Q: What do you mean by eligible to enroll?
>
> A: By eligible we mean does your employer provide such coverage? Could you sign up for it either now or during the last or next open enrollment period?

14. Does your employer offer an explicit incentive not to enroll in their health plan, such as a monetary bonus?

   a. Yes (ask 14B)

   b. No

14B. Does this incentive apply specifically to TRICARE eligible employees?

    a. Yes

    b. No

IF MARSTAT=0 AND Q12=0, SKIP TO Q19

15. Are you currently <u>eligible</u> to enroll your [[spouse/partner]/dependents/[spouse/partner] and dependents] in your employer plan? IF THE R SAYS [SPOUSE/PARTNER] CAN ENROLL BUT NOT DEPENDENTS OR [SPOUSE/PARTNETR] CANNOT ENROLL BUT DEPENDENTS CAN, CODE YES

    `a. Yes

    b. No

Q: What do you mean by eligible to enroll?

A: By eligible we mean does your employer provide such coverage? Could you sign up for it either now or during the last or next open enrollment period?

IF MARSTATUS=0, 1 SKIP TO 19

16. Is your [spouse/partner] currently <u>eligible</u> to enroll in a health insurance plan offered by his/her employer?

    a. Yes

    b. No (skip to Q. 19)

Q: What do you mean by eligible to enroll?

A: By eligible we mean does the employer provide such coverage? Could your [spouse/partner] sign up for it either now or during the last or next open enrollment period?

---

17. Are you currently <u>eligible</u> to enroll yourself {and your dependents} in this plan? IF THE R SAYS THEY CAN ENROLL BUT NOT THE DEPENDENTS OR THEY CANNOT ENROLL BUT DEPENDENTS CAN, CODE YES

    a. Yes

    b. No

SEE Q&A FOR QUESTION 16.

18. Does your [spouse/partner]'s employer offer an explicit incentive not to enroll in their health plan, such as a monetary bonus?

    a. Yes (ask 18B)

    b. No

18B. Does this incentive apply specifically to TRICARE eligible employees?

    a. Yes

    b. No

19. Are you {or your [spouse/partner]} currently eligible to enroll in a health insurance plan offered through any other civilian source, not including TRICARE? For example, through a union or professional association that you {or your [spouse/partner]} belong to. I am now referring to sources other than health insurance provided by employers.

    a. Yes (IF Q12=0 AND MARSTATUS=0, SKIP TO 21 AND CODE Q20a AS "YES")

    b. No (skip to Q. 21)

Q: What do you mean by eligible to enroll?

A: By eligible we mean does the plan provide such coverage? Could you sign up for it either now or during the last or next open enrollment period?

20. a. Are you eligible to enroll in such a plan? (Yes   No)   (IF MARSTATUS=0, SKIP TO 20c)

    b. Is your [spouse/partner] eligible to enroll in such a plan? (Yes   No)

    (IF Q12=0 SKIP TO 21)

    c. Are your dependents eligible to enroll in such a plan? (Yes   No)

21. Now I would like to ask you about the civilian health insurance plans in which you {and your family} are currently enrolled (Do not include participation in TRICARE). I am talking about health care coverage, not enrollment in dental or vision plans.

OPTIONS FOR WHICH THE RESPONDENT, [SPOUSE/PARTNER], OR DEPENDENTS WERE NOT ELIGIBLE TO ENROLL SHOULD NOT APPEAR BELOW. THUS, FOR EXAMPLE:

- IF Q1="NO," QUESTION 21a SHOULD NOT APPEAR

- IF MARSTAT=1 OR MARSTAT=0, QUESTION 21b SHOULD NOT APPEAR

- IF Q19="NO," QUESTION 21c SHOULD NOT APPEAR

- IF MARSTAT=0 AND Q12=0, COLUMN B AND QUESTION 21b SHOULD NOT APPEAR

- IF MARSTAT=0 AND Q12=1, COLUMN B SHOULD NOT ASK ABOUT [SPOUSE/PARTNER]

- IF MARSTAT=1 AND Q12=0, COLUMN B SHOULD NOT ASK ABOUT DEPENDENTS

(Mark all that apply)

	Are you currently enrolled in? A	Are your [spouse/partner] or your dependents currently enrolled in? B
a. Health coverage provided by your employer		
b. Health coverage provided through your spouse's employer		
c. Health coverage provided through a union or professional association		
d. Health coverage purchased directly from an insurance company		
e. Health coverage from the Veteran's Administration (VA)		
f. Other non-TRICARE civilian coverage (for example, COBRA coverage through former employer or coverage obtained through enrollment in a school or university)		

CREATE FOUR VARIABLES CALLED SELF_ELIGIBLE, SELF_ENROLLED, FAM_ELIGIBLE AND FAM_ENROLLED

1. SELF_ELIGIBLE=0

    SELF_ELIGIBLE=1 IF Q13="YES" OR Q17="YES" OR Q20A="YES"

2. FAM_ELIGIBLE=0

    FAM_ELIGIBLE=N/A IF MARSTAT=0 AND Q12=0

    FAM_ELIGIBLE=1 IF Q15="YES" OR Q16="YES" OR (Q12>0 AND Q17="YES") OR (Q20b="YES" OR Q20c="YES")

3. SELF_ENROLLED= N/A IF SELF_ELIGIBLE=0

    SELF_ENROLLED=0 IF RESPONDENT ANSWERED "NO" TO EVERY BOX IN Q21, COLUMN A

    SELF_ENROLLED=1 IF ANY BOX IN COLUMN A IS MARKED "YES"

4. FAM_ENROLLED= N/A IF FAM_ELIGIBLE= N/A OR FAM_ELIGIBLE=0

    FAM_ENROLLED=0 IF MARSTAT ≠ 0 AND RESPONDENT ANSWERED "NO" TO EVERY BOX IN Q21, COLUMN B

    FAM_ENROLLED=1 IF ANY BOX IN COLUMN B IS MARKED "YES"

SKIP PATTERNS FOR QUESTIONS 22 THROUGH 31 ARE NOTED IN THE TABLE BELOW

IN QUESTIONS 22-27, PLEASE NOTE THAT THE WORDS "YOU" OR "YOU AND YOUR FAMILY" OR "YOUR FAMILY MEMBERS" WILL APPEAR DEPENDING ON THE FOLLOWING:

SELF_ELIGIBLE	FAM_ELIGIBLE	SELF_ENROLLED	FAM_ENROLLED	WORDING AND SKIP PATTERN FOR Q22-31
=1	N/A	=1	N/A	SKIP Q22-25 "YOU" IN Q26-27
=1	N/A	=0	N/A	"YOU' IN Q22-25 SKIP Q26-31
=0	N/A	N/A	N/A	SKIP Q22 "YOU" IN Q23-25 SKIP Q26-31
=1	=1	=1	=1	SKIP Q22-25 "YOU AND YOUR FAMILY" IN Q26-27
=1	=1	=1	=0	"YOUR FAMILY MEMBERS" IN Q22-25 "YOU" IN Q26-27
=1	=1	=0	=1	"YOU" IN Q22-25 "YOUR FAMILY MEMBERS" IN Q26-27
=1	=1	=0	=0	"YOU AND YOUR FAMILY" IN Q22-25 SKIP Q26-31
=1	=0	=1	N/A	SKIP Q22 "YOUR FAMILY MEMBERS" IN Q23-25 "YOU" IN Q26-27
=1	=0	=0	N/A	"YOU" IN Q22 "YOU AND YOUR FAMILY IN Q23-25 SKIP Q26-31
=0	=1	N/A	=1	SKIP Q22 "YOU" IN Q23-25 "YOUR FAMILY MEMBERS" IN Q26-27

=0	=1	N/A	=0	"YOUR FAMILY MEMBERS" IN Q22 "YOU AND YOUR FAMILY" IN Q23-25 SKIP Q26-31
=0	=0	N/A	N/A	SKIP Q22 "YOU AND YOUR FAMILY" IN Q23-25 SKIP Q26-31

22. What were the reasons why [you/you and your family/your family members] are not currently enrolled in the non-TRICARE civilian insurance for which [you/you and your family/your family members] are eligible? I am going to read you a list and for each item, please tell me whether that was a reason or not for not enrolling.

   a. Premium contributions too expensive (Yes   No)

   b. Does not cover the medical care [you/you and your family/your family members] need (Yes   No)

   c. High co-pays or co-insurance (Yes   No)

   d. High deductibles (Yes   No)

   e. Cannot choose doctors or hospitals (Yes   No)

   f. Prefer doctors in Military Treatment Facilities or in TRICARE (Yes   No)

   g. Employer provided incentive to use military coverage (Yes   No)

   h. Paperwork, administrative burden, or delays in reimbursement (Yes   No)

   i. Any other reasons? Specify _____

23. At any time since you retired from DoD, have [you/you and your family/your family members] ever been enrolled in a non-TRICARE civilian health insurance plan such as an employer plan or a plan offered through a professional association?

   a. Yes

   b. No (skip Q24 and Q25)

24. Approximately how many years has it been since [you/you and your family/your family members] were enrolled in this plan?

    a.   1 to 2

    b.   3 to 4

    c.   5 to 6

    d.   6 to 10

    e.   More than 10 years

25. Why did [you/you and your family/your family members] decide to discontinue participation in the non-TRICARE civilian plan?

    a.   The plan became too expensive (Yes   No)

    b.   A job change eliminated your access to this plan (Yes   No)

    c.   The plan is no longer offered (Yes   No)

    d.   You became dissatisfied with the medical care received in this plan (Yes   No)

    e.   Paperwork, administrative burden, and delays in reimbursement (Yes   No)

    f.   The plan denied care you thought was necessary (Yes   No)

    g.   Employer provided incentive to use military coverage (Yes   No)

    h.   Any other reasons? Specify _____

26. What were the reasons why [you/you and your family/your family members] chose to enroll in a civilian health insurance plan? I am going to read you a list and for each item, please tell me whether that was a reason for enrolling.

    a.   Eligible for free coverage through employer, spouse's employer, or other non-TRICARE source (Yes   No)

    b.   Civilian coverage is less costly than TRICARE for [you/you and your family/your family members] (Yes   No)   IF YES:

         •   Are civilian co-pays or co-insurance less costly? (Yes   No)

- Are civilian deductibles lower? (Yes   No)

- Is the civilian premium lower? (Yes   No)

c. Prefer the network of doctors and hospitals in civilian plan (Yes   No)

d. Prefer <u>not</u> to receive care at a Military Treatment Facility (Yes   No)

e. Military Treatment Facilities are not conveniently located (Yes   No)

f. TRICARE does not cover the medical care that I need (Yes   No)

g. Dissatisfied with care received through TRICARE (Yes   No)

h. Paperwork, administrative burden, or delays in reimbursement (Yes   No)

i. TRICARE has denied care you thought was necessary (Yes   No)

j. Any other reasons? Specify _____

Q: What is a deductible?

A: A deductible is the amount an individual must pay for health care expenses before insurance covers any further costs. Plans typically have a yearly deductible, and the size of the deductible may vary depending on whether the individual has single or family coverage.

Q: What is co-insurance?

A: Co-insurance refers to money that an individual is required to pay for services, after a deductible has been paid. In some health care plans, co-insurance is called "co-payment." Co-insurance is often specified by a percentage. For example, the employee pays 20 percent toward the charges for a service and the employer or insurance company pays 80 percent.

Q: What is a co-payment?

A: A co-payment is a predetermined (flat) fee that an individual pays for health care services, in addition to what the insurance covers. For example, some HMOs require a $10 "co-payment" for each office visit, regardless of the type or level of services provided during the visit. Co-payments are not usually specified by percentages.

27. For the non-TRICARE civilian health care plan in which [you/you and your family/your family members] are enrolled, do you {or your [spouse/partner]} have to pay some or all of the insurance premium (for example, through payroll deductions)?

    a. Yes

    b. No (skip to Q. 32)

I'd like to ask you about the amount [you/you and your family/your family members] personally spend for non-TRICARE health insurance premiums. Please include payroll deductions for premiums. (Answer in whichever time period is most convenient). {IF MARSTAT > 0 OR Q12 > 0: Include premiums only for coverage for yourself and any family members who are eligible for retiree medical benefits under TRICARE.}

Q: What do you mean by premium contribution?

A: The employee premium contribution is the amount of money that you must pay annually to purchase health insurance for yourself and your dependents. Typically, your share of the premium is deducted from your paycheck before taxes are taken from your gross pay. Sometimes the employee premium contribution is referred to as an "enrollment fee."

---

28. What was the amount?

    i. $_____

    ii. Don't know (skip to Q. 30)

29. Over what time period?

    a. Weekly (skip to Q. 31)

    b. Every two weeks (skip to Q. 31)

    c. Twice a month (skip to Q. 31)

    d. Monthly (skip to Q. 31)

    e. Quarterly (skip to Q. 31)

    f. Twice a year (skip to Q. 31)

    g.   Yearly (skip to Q. 31)

    h.   DON'T KNOW

30. Can you give me an estimate of the annual premium? Was it:

- Zero
- $1-249
- $250-499
- $500-1499
- $1500-2499
- $2500-3999
- $4000 or more
- DON'T KNOW

31. The premium that you just gave me, is that for health care only or for dental and or vision coverage as well?

    a.   Health care only

    b.   Dental/vision included

32. In calendar year 2005, how much "out-of-pocket" money did you and other family members who were eligible for retiree medical benefits spend on medical care that was not reimbursed by any health insurance plan? Do not include cost of health insurance premiums, over the counter remedies, dental or vision related-expenses, or any costs for which you expect to get reimbursed.

    a.   Zero

    b.   Less than $500

    c. $501-1999

    d. $2000-2999

    e. $3000-4999

f. $5000 or more

g.   DON'T KNOW

Q: What do you mean by "out-of-pocket" expenses?

A: "Out-of-Pocket" expenses refer to the total dollar value of all co-payments, co-insurance payments, health care deductibles—the total amount for all health care plans, both TRICARE and non-TRICARE.

Participation in and Use of TRICARE

33. In calendar year 2005, did you {or your family} receive any medical care at any of the following facilities or clinics? (Do not include any medical care paid for under Workmen's Compensation or similar coverage)

IF MARSTAT=0 AND Q12=0, SECOND RESPONSE COLUMN SHOULD NOT APPEAR

	You	Your Family
a. A military facility (i.e. military clinic, military hospital, Military Treatment Facilities)		
b. A civilian facility (i.e. doctor's office, clinic, hospital, civilian TRICARE contractor)		
c. Other facility (such as a Veterans Affairs clinic or hospital or Uniformed Services Family Health Plan facility)		

34. Thinking about the medical care you {and your family} received in calendar year 2005, what health insurance coverage did you rely on to provide this care? This <u>does not</u> include prescriptions that you may have filled for yourself or family members. (CHECK ALL THAT APPLY)

    a. TRICARE (including care received at MTFs)

    b. Non-TRICARE civilian plan

    c. VA coverage

    d. No medical care received or no medical care paid for by any of these sources

35. Thinking about any prescriptions that you {and your family} may have filled in calendar year 2005, what health insurance coverage did you rely on to provide this care? (CHECK ALL THAT APPLY)

    a. TRICARE (including prescriptions filled at MTFs)

    b. Non-TRICARE civilian plan

    c. VA coverage

    d. No prescriptions filled or no prescriptions paid for by any of these sources

<u>Health Care Status</u>

36. Would you say your health in general is:

    a. Excellent

    b. Very good

    c. Good

    d. Fair

    e. Poor

NOTE TO PROGRAMMER: SKIP Q37 IF MARSTAT=0 AND Q12=0

37. Please think about family members who are eligible for retiree medical benefits under TRICARE.

A. In calendar year 2005, whose health concerned you the most or who required medical care the most?

    a. You (skip Q36B)

    b. Your spouse or partner

    c. Dependent family member

B. Would you say this person's health in general is:

    a. Excellent

    b. Very good

    c. Good

    d. Fair

    e. Poor

IF NO ELIGIBILITY FOR CIVILIAN COVERAGE (OR ENROLLMENT RESPONSES MISSING),

    (SELF_ENROLLED=N/A) AND (FAM_ENROLLED=N/A),

        END SURVEY.

IF NO ENROLLMENT IN CIVILIAN COVERAGE GIVEN ELIGIBILITY,

    (SELF_ENROLLED=0) AND (FAM_ENROLLED=N/A), OR

    (SELF_ENROLLED=N/A) AND (FAM_ENROLLED=0), OR

    (SELF_ENROLLED=0) AND (FAM_ENROLLED=0),

        SKIP TO Q39.

IF FULL ENROLLMENT IN CIVILIAN COVERAGE GIVEN ELIGIBILITY,

(SELF_ENROLLED=1) AND (FAM_ENROLLED=N/A), OR

(SELF_ENROLLED=N/A) AND (FAM_ENROLLED=1), OR

(SELF_ENROLLED=1) AND (FAM_ENROLLED=1) ,

IF PREMIUM PAID (Q27 = YES), CONTINUE TO Q38;

ELSE, END SURVEY.

IF PARTIAL ENROLLMENT IN CIVILIAN COVERAGE GIVEN ELIGIBILITY

(SELF_ENROLLED=1) AND (FAM_ENROLLED=0), OR

(SELF_ENROLLED=0) AND (FAM_ENROLLED=1),

IF PREMIUM PAID (Q27 = YES), CONTINUE TO Q38;

ELSE, CONTINUE TO Q39.

Some Options

38. [you/you and your family/your family members] are currently enrolled in a non-TRICARE health insurance plan. Would [you/you and your family/your family members] give up this enrollment in favor of TRICARE if your premium contributions to the civilian plan(s) rose by 25%? NOTE TO INTERVIEWER: IF RESPONDENT IS RELUCTANT TO ANSWER, PLEASE PROMPT HIM/HER TO RESPOND BASED ON "BEST GUESS". IF RESPONDENT OFFERS COMMENTS, PLEASE PROMPT TO RESPOND AND ALSO CODE COMMENTS IN SPACE PROVIDED BELOW.

    a. Yes

    b. No

    IF COMMENTS ARE OFFERED, CODE HERE: _____

IF FULL ENROLLMENT IN CIVILIAN COVERAGE GIVEN ELIGIBILITY,

(SELF_ENROLLED=1) AND (FAM_ENROLLED=N/A), OR

(SELF_ENROLLED=N/A) AND (FAM_ENROLLED=1), OR

(SELF_ENROLLED=1) AND (FAM_ENROLLED=1) ,

END SURVEY.

39. [you/you and your family/your family members] are currently eligible, but not enrolled, in a non-TRICARE civilian health insurance plan. Would [you/you and your family/your family members] enroll in this plan if your premium contributions to the non-TRICARE civilian plan(s) decreased by 25%? NOTE TO INTERVIEWER: IF RESPONDENT IS RELUCTANT TO ANSWER, PLEASE PROMPT HIM/HER TO RESPOND BASED ON "BEST GUESS". IF RESPONDENT OFFERS COMMENTS, PLEASE PROMPT TO RESPOND AND ALSO CODE COMMENTS IN SPACE PROVIDED BELOW.

    a. Yes

    b. No

IF COMMENTS ARE OFFERED, CODE HERE: _____

END SURVEY.

95% Confidence Intervals for Figures in Chapters Three Through Six

Supporting Tables for Chapter Three

Table B.1
95% Confidence Intervals for Percentage of Military Retirees Who Were Employed, February–March 2006 (Figure 3.2)

Age	Estimate 95% Confidence Intervals (lower bound, upper bound)
≤45 years	89.7 (82.8, 96.6)
46–50 years	93.8 (90.0, 97.6)
51–55 years	87.0 (81.3, 92.6)
56–60 years	79.5 (73.1, 85.9)
61–64 years	52.6 (43.6, 61.9)

Table B.2
95% Confidence Intervals for Percentage of Retired Officers and Enlisted Personnel Employed by Different Types of Employer (Figure 3.3)

Type of Employer	Officers	Enlisted Personnel	Total
	Estimate 95% Confidence Intervals (lower bound, upper bound)		
Not employed	22.0 (18.3, 25.7)	19.6 (15.8, 23.3)	20.1 (17.1, 23.1)
Government	21.7 (18.1, 25.2)	22.6 (18.5, 26.7)	22.3 (19.1, 25.6)
Private-sector firm	40.9 (36.7, 45.2)	50.0 (45.1, 54.8)	47.8 (44.0, 51.7)
Self-employed	10.6 (7.9, 13.4)	4.5 (2.5, 6.6)	6.0 (4.3, 7.7)
More than one employer	4.8 (3.0, 6.5)	3.4 (1.6, 5.1)	3.7 (2.3, 5.1)

Table B.3
95% Confidence Intervals for Percentage of Employed Retired Officers and Enlisted Personnel Who Were Working Full Time in February–March 2006, by Age Group (Figure 3.4)

Age	Officers	Enlisted Personnel	Total
	Estimate 95% Confidence Intervals (lower bound, upper bound)		
≤ 60 years	90.3 (87.2, 93.3)	95.3 (92.8, 97.7)	94.2 (92.2, 96.2)
61–64 years	73.7 (62.0, 85.5)	68.6 (52.4, 85.7)	70.3 (58.3, 82.3)

Table B.4
95% Confidence Intervals for Percentage of Retired Officers and Enlisted Personnel Employed by Different-Sized Firms (Figure 3.5)

Size of Employer	Officers	Enlisted Personnel	Total
	Estimate 95% Confidence Intervals (lower bound, upper bound)		
1–9 workers	15.0 (11.4, 18.6)	8.8 (5.8, 11.9)	10.2 (7.7, 12.8)
10–24 workers	2.3 (0.9, 3.8)	6.5 (3.8, 9.1)	5.5 (3.4, 7.6)
25–99 workers	6.6 (4.2, 8.9)	10.0 (6.7, 13.2)	9.2 (6.6, 11.7)
100–199 workers	6.0 (3.7, 8.3)	7.7 (4.9, 10.6)	7.3 (5.1, 9.6)
200–499 workers	7.3 (4.9, 9.6)	8.9 (5.9, 12.0)	8.5 (6.1, 11.0)
500 or more workers	59.4 (54.6, 64.2)	52.8 (47.4, 58.3)	54.3 (50.0, 58.7)

Table B.5
95% Confidence Intervals for Percentage of Spouses of Retired Officers and Enlisted Personnel Employed by Different Types of Employer (Figure 3.6)

Type of Employer	Spouses of Officers	Spouses of Enlisted Personnel	Total
	Estimate 95% Confidence Intervals (lower bound, upper bound)		
Not employed	45.7 (41.1, 50.3)	37.5 (32.6, 42.4)	39.5 (35.6, 43.4)
Government	16.9 (13.5, 20.2)	16.3 (12.5, 20.2)	16.4 (13.4, 19.5)
Private-sector firm	28.8 (24.6,33.0)	39.2 (34.2, 44.2)	36.7 (32.7, 40.6)
Self-employed	6.6 (4.3, 9.0)	4.0 (1.9, 6.0)	4.6 (3.0, 6.2)
More than one employer	2.1 (0.7, 3.4)	3.1 (1.3, 4.8)	2.8 (1.4, 4.2)

Table B.6
95% Confidence Intervals for Percentage of Spouses of Retired Officers and Enlisted Personnel Employed by Different-Sized Firms (Figure 3.7)

Size of Employer	Spouses of Officers	Spouses of Enlisted Personnel	Total
	Estimate 95% Confidence Intervals (lower bound, upper bound)		
1–9 workers	19.5 (14.5, 24.6)	13.1 (8.6, 17.7)	14.5 (10.8, 18.3)
10–24 workers	7.7 (4.4, 10.9)	5.7 (2.7, 8.8)	6.2 (3.7, 8.6)
25–99 workers	8.5 (4.8, 12.3)	11.0 (6.9, 15.1)	10.5 (7.2, 13.8)
100–199 workers	4.5 (1.9, 7.0)	6.2 (3.1, 9.3)	5.8 (3.3, 8.3)
200–499 workers	9.8 (6.2, 13.3)	5.6 (2.4, 8.7)	6.5 (3.9, 9.0)
500 or more workers	45.9 (39.7, 52.1)	49.5 (43.1, 56.0)	48.7 (43.5, 53.9)

Table B.7
95% Confidence Intervals for Percentage of Retired Officers and Enlisted Personnel, by Number of Dependents Eligible for TRICARE Benefits as of February–March 2006 (Figure 3.8)

	Officers	Enlisted Personnel	Total
Number of dependents	Estimate 95% Confidence Intervals (lower bound, upper bound)		
None	61.8 (57.9, 65.7)	65.1 (60.6, 69.5)	64.3 (60.8, 67.8)
One	15.5 (12.5, 18.5)	15.5 (12.0, 18.0)	15.5 (12.7, 18.2)
Two	15.4 (12.4, 18.4)	14.2 (10.8, 17.5)	14.5 (11.8, 17.1)
Three or more	7.0 (5.0, 9.1)	5.3 (3.1, 7.4)	5.7 (4.0, 7.4)

Table B.8
95% Confidence Intervals for Percentage of Retirees, by Annual Household Income and Employment Status (Figure 3.9)

	Officers		Enlisted Personnel	
	Employed	Not Employed	Employed	Not Employed
Annual Household Income	Estimate 95% Confidence Intervals (lower bound, upper bound)			
≤$25,000	0.3 (0.0, 0.8)	0.8 (0.0, 2.3)	4.8 (2.5, 7.2)	21.1 (12.3, 29.8)
$25,001–$50,000	5.7 (3.3, 8.1)	21.5 (12.7, 30.3)	20.8 (16.3, 25.2)	39.7 (28.4, 51.0)
$50,001–$75,000	7.1 (4.4, 9.8)	26.1 (16.3, 35.9)	30.1 (25.1, 35.1)	21.4 (11.8, 31.0)
$75,001–$100,000	14.9 (11.5, 18.3)	19.5 (10.2, 28.8)	18.7 (14.5, 22.9)	2.5 (0.0, 5.9)
Over $100,000	66.5 (61.8, 71.1)	28.1 (18.5, 37.7)	17.5 (13.3, 21.6)	6.9 (0.8, 13.0)

Supporting Tables for Chapter Four

Table B.9
95% Confidence Intervals for Percentage of Military Retirees and Families with Access to Different Sources of Civilian Health Insurance, February–March 2006 (Figures 4.1 and 4.2)

Types of Civilian Health Insurance Plans for Which Retirees or Families Are Eligible	Retirees	Retirees with Families
	Estimate 95% Confidence Intervals (lower bound, upper bound)	
None	24.1 (20.8, 27.3)	21.5 (18.3, 24.8)
Own employer only	35.5 (31.8, 39.2)	30.9 (27.2, 34.5)
Own and spouse's employer	20.6 (17.4, 23.7)	24.9 (21.4, 28.4)
Own employer and non-employer source	5.3 (3.6, 6.9)	4.1 (2.5, 5.6)
All three sources	4.5 (2.9, 6.1)	4.3 (2.7, 6.0)
Spouse's employer only	5.6 (3.8, 7.4)	10.0 (7.5, 12.5)
Non-employer source	3.8 (2.3, 5.4)	3.3 (1.8, 4.9)
Spouse's employer and non-employer source	0.7 (0.1, 1.4)	1.0 (0.2, 1.8)

Table B.10
95% Confidence Intervals for Percentage of Military Retirees Reporting Eligibility for Employer Health Insurance, by Size of Employer, February–March 2006 (Figure 4.3)

Firm Size	Estimate 95% Confidence Intervals (lower bound, upper bound)
1–9 workers	22.5 (11.8, 33.3)
10–24 workers	61.2 (41.6, 80.8)
25–99 workers	92.6 (76.4, 94.3)
100–199 workers	91.7 (78.1, 97.2)
200–499 workers	81.0 (66.5, 90.2)
500 or more workers	92.6 (88.7, 95.2)

Table B.11
95% Confidence Intervals for Percentage of Military Retirees Reporting Eligibility for Employer Health Insurance, by Type of Employer, February–March 2006 (Figure 4.4)

Type of Employer	Estimate 95% Confidence Intervals (lower bound, upper bound)
Government	96.7 (93.8, 99.6)
Private-sector firm	84.7 (80.6, 88.9)
Self-employed	20.9 (9.1, 32.6)
More than one employer	67.6 (49.2, 85.9)

Supporting Tables for Chapter Five

Table B.12
95% Confidence Intervals for Percentage of Retired Officers and Enlisted Personnel Enrolled in Civilian Health Insurance Plans for Self-Coverage, February–March 2006 (Figure 5.1)

	Officers	Enlisted Personnel	Total
Non-TRICARE Civilian Health Coverage in Which Retiree Was Enrolled	Estimate 95% Confidence Intervals (lower bound, upper bound)		
Not enrolled in a civilian plan	62.7 (58.5, 67.0)	65.8 (61.1, 70.4)	65.0 (61.3, 68.8)
Enrolled in one civilian plan	32.4 (28.3, 36.5)	29.9 (25.4, 34.5)	30.5 (26.9, 34.1)
Enrolled in two or more civilian plans	4.9 (3.0, 6.7)	4.3 (2.4, 6.3)	4.4 (2.9, 6.0)

Table B.13
95% Confidence Intervals for Percentage of Retired Officers and Enlisted Personnel, by Enrollment in Civilian Health Insurance Plans for Family Coverage for Spouse/Dependents, February–March 2006 (Figure 5.2)

	Officers	Enlisted Personnel	Total
Non-TRICARE Civilian Health Coverage in Which Spouse/Dependent Was Enrolled	Estimate 95% Confidence Intervals (lower bound, upper bound)		
Family not enrolled in a civilian plan	54.1 (49.7, 58.6)	54.9 (50.0, 59.9)	54.8 (50.8, 58.7)
Enrolled in one civilian plan	31.4 (27.3 35.5)	32.0 (27.4, 36.6)	31.8 (28.2, 35.5)
Enrolled in two or more civilian plans	7.4 (5.2, 9.7)	4.6 (2.6, 6.6)	5.2 (3.6, 6.9)

Table B.14
95% Confidence Intervals for Percentage of Retired Officers and Enlisted Personnel with Families, by Type of Health Insurance Coverage, February–March 2006 (Figure 5.3)

Non-TRICARE Civilian Health Coverage in Which Spouse/Dependent Was Enrolled	Officers	Enlisted Personnel	Total
	Estimate 95% Confidence Intervals (lower bound, upper bound)		
No other health coverage	55.6 (51.1, 60.1)	56.3 (51.1, 61.4)	56.1 (52.1, 60.2)
Self-coverage only	2.5 (1.2, 3.9)	3.8 (1.8, 5.7)	3.5 (2.0, 5.0)
Family coverage only	5.7 (3.8, 7.7)	8.6 (5.6, 11.5)	7.9 (5.6, 10.2)
Both self- and family coverage	36.2 (31.8, 40.6)	31.4 (26.6, 36.1)	32.5 (28.7, 36.3)

Table B.15
95% Confidence Intervals for Percentage of Military Retirees Not Enrolled in Civilian Health Insurance Plans for Which They are Eligible, by Reason for Non-enrollment, February–March 2006 (Figure 5.4)

Reason for Non-enrollment	Estimate 95% Confidence Intervals (lower bound, upper bound)
Premium contributions too expensive	78.2 (73.4, 82.9)
High copays or coinsurance	58.3 (52.5, 64.0)
High deductibles	57.4 (51.5, 63.3)
Prefer doctors in MTFs or TRICARE	50.9 (45.0, 56.9)
Cannot choose doctors/hospital	29.4 (24.0, 34.7)
Does not cover needed medical care	21.5 (16.5, 26.5)
Paperwork, administrative burden, reimbursement delays	12.0 (8.2, 15.7)
Employer provided incentive to use military coverage	5.1 (2.5, 7.6)

Table B.16
95% Confidence Intervals for Percentage of Military Retirees Previously Enrolled in Civilian Health Insurance Plans, by Reason for Discontinuing Enrollment, February–March 2006 (Figure 5.5)

Reason for Non-enrollment	Estimate 95% Confidence Intervals (lower bound, upper bound)
Plan became too expensive	47.5 (39.8, 55.2)
Job change eliminated access to plan	44.7 (37.1, 52.3)
Plan no longer offered	19.8 (13.7, 25.9)
Became dissatisfied with medical care received under plan	9.6 (5.1, 14.1)
Plan denied necessary care	8.7 (4.4, 12.9)
Paperwork, administrative burden, reimbursement delays	8.5 (4.5, 12.4)
Employer provided incentive to use military coverage	4.1 (1.3, 7.0)

Table B.17
95% Confidence Intervals for Percentage of Retired Officers and Enlisted Personnel Currently Enrolled in Civilian Health Insurance Plans, by Reason for Enrollment, February–March 2006 (Figure 5.6)

Reason for Enrollment	Estimate 95% Confidence Intervals (lower bound, upper bound)
Prefer network of doctors/hospitals in civilian plan	51.8 (45.8, 57.7)
MTFs not conveniently located	48.5 (42.6, 54.4)
Eligible for free coverage (own or spouse's employer, other non-TRICARE source)	29.9 (24.5, 35.3)
TRICARE does not cover needed medical care	25.6 (20.3, 30.9)
Paperwork, administrative burden, reimbursement delays	25.2 (20.1, 30.2)
Civilian coverage less costly than TRICARE	20.7 (15.9, 25.5)
Prefer not to receive care at MTFs	20.0 (15.3, 24.7)
TRICARE denied coverage for needed care	13.2 (9.2, 17.2)

Supporting Tables for Chapter Six

Table B.18
95% Confidence Intervals for Percentage of Retired Officers and Enlisted Personnel, by Type of Facility Where They Received Medical Care in 2005, February–March 2006 (Figure 6.1)

Type of Facility	Officers	Enlisted Personnel	Total Population
	Estimate 95% Confidence Intervals (lower bound, upper bound)		
Military facility only	15.9 (12.9, 19.0)	11.8 (8.6, 14.9)	12.8 (10.2, 15.3)
Civilian facility only	45.2 (40.8, 49.7)	38.7 (34.0, 43.4)	40.2 (36.5, 44.0)
Other facility (VA clinic, USFHP clinic)	2.3 (1.1, 3.5)	6.1 (3.8, 8.4)	5.2 (3.4, 7.0)
Military and civilian facility	17.8 (14.4, 21.3)	14.5 (11.0, 17.9)	15.2 (12.5, 18.0)
Military and other facility	2.0 (0.9, 3.1)	4.8 (2.7, 7.0)	4.2 (2.5, 5.8)
Civilian and other facility	5.5 (3.5, 7.4)	8.5 (5.7, 11.3)	7.8 (5.6, 10.0)
All three facilities	2.4 (1.3, 4.6)	6.0 (3.6, 8.4)	5.2 (3.3, 7.0)
No medical care received	8.8 (6.5, 11.8)	9.7 (6.8, 12.5)	9.5 (7.2, 11.7)

Table B.19
95% Confidence Intervals for Percentage of Families of Retired Officers and Enlisted Personnel, by Type of Facility Where They Received Medical Care in 2005, February–March 2006 (Figure 6.2)

Type of Facility	Families of Officers	Families of Enlisted Personnel	Total Population
	Estimate 95% Confidence Intervals (lower bound, upper bound)		
No spouse/dependents	7.1 (4.5, 9.6)	8.5 (5.7, 11.3)	8.2 (6.0, 10.4)
Military facility only	10.4 (7.9, 12.9)	10.2 (7.3, 13.1)	10.3 (8.0, 12.6)
Civilian facility only	51.8 (47.4, 56.2)	47.3 (42.4, 52.2)	48.4 (44.5, 52.2)
Other facility (VA clinic, USFHP clinic)	0.6 (0.0, 1.2)	0.2 (0.0, 0.7)	0.3 (0.0, 0.7)
Military and civilian facility	20.7 (17.2, 24.2)	18.3 (14.5, 22.1)	18.8 (15.8, 21.9)
Military and other facility	0.8 (0.0, 1.7)	1.0 (0.0, 1.9)	0.9 (0.2, 1.7)
Civilian and other facility	1.2 (0.3, 2.2)	3.1 (1.3, 4.8)	2.7 (1.3, 4.0)
All three facilities	1.8 (0.8, 2.9)	1.7 (0.4, 2.9)	1.7 (0.7, 2.7)
No medical care received	5.6 (3.3, 7.9)	9.7 (6.8, 12.6)	8.2 (6.5, 11.0)

Table B.20
95% Confidence Intervals for Percentage of Retired Officers and Enlisted Personnel, by Enrollment in Civilian Plan and Type of Health Insurance Coverage Used for Medical Care in 2005, February–March 2006 (Figures 6.3 and 6.4)

	Officers		Enlisted Personnel		Total Population	
	Enrolled in Civilian Plan	Not Enrolled in Civilian Plan	Enrolled in Civilian Plan	Not Enrolled in Civilian Plan	Enrolled in Civilian Plan	Not Enrolled in Civilian Plan
Type of Health Insurance Coverage	Estimate 95% Confidence Intervals (lower bound, upper bound)					
TRICARE only	10.6 (6.3, 14.9)	82.8 (78.1, 87.6)	7.0 (3.2, 10.9)	70.7 (64.7, 76.6)	7.9 (4.8, 11.0)	73.5 (68.8, 78.2)
Non-TRICARE civilian plan only	40.2 (33.6, 46.8)	1.7 (0.2, 3.1)	37.3 (30.0, 44.6)	2.9 (0.8, 5.0)	38.0 (32.2, 43.8)	2.6 (1.0, 4.3)
VA coverage only	0 —	1.2 (0.0, 2.3)	1.7 (0.0, 3.7)	4.3 (1.7, 6.9)	1.3 (0.0, 2.8)	3.5 (1.5, 5.5)
TRICARE and non-TRICARE civilian plan	39.3 (32.6, 45.9)	5.1 (2.1, 8.0)	34.7 (27.5, 41.9)	4.2 (1.5, 6.9)	35.8 (30.1, 41.5)	4.4 (2.2, 6.6)
TRICARE and VA coverage	1.2 (0.0, 2.5)	6.8 (3.7, 9.9)	3.4 (0.7, 6.2)	12.9 (8.5, 17.3)	2.9 (0.8, 5.0)	11.5 (8.1, 14.9)
Non-TRICARE civilian plan and VA coverage	5.1 (2.1, 8.1)	0.3 (0.0, 0.9)	10.7 (6.0, 15.4)	0 —	9.3 (5.7, 13.0)	0.1 (0.0, 0.2)
All three sources	2.0 (0.3, 3.7)	0.4 (0.0, 1.1)	5.2 (1.9, 8.5)	3.4 (1.1, 5.8)	4.4 (1.9, 6.9)	2.7 (0.9, 4.5)
No medical care received/paid for by any of these sources	1.6 (0.0, 3.6)	1.8 (0.0, 3.9)	0 —	1.7 (0.0, 3.3)	0.4 (0.0, 0.8)	1.7 (0.4, 3.0)

Table B.21
95% Confidence Intervals for Percentage of Retired Officers and Enlisted Personnel Enrolled in Civilian Plan, by Type of Health Insurance Coverage Used to Pay for Prescriptions in 2005, February–March 2006 (Figure 6.5)

Type of Health Insurance Coverage	Officers	Enlisted Personnel	Total Population
	Estimate 95% Confidence Intervals (lower bound, upper bound)		
TRICARE only	19.3 (13.8, 24.8)	18.7 (12.7, 24.7)	18.8 (14.0, 23.6)
Non-TRICARE civilian plan only	40.1 (33.8, 46.4)	30.4 (23.4, 37.3)	32.7 (27.1, 38.2)
VA coverage only	0 —	3.4 (0.7, 6.1)	2.6 (0.6, 4.7)
TRICARE and non-TRICARE civilian plan	34.2 (27.6, 40.9)	30.1 (23.0, 37.2)	31.1 (25.4, 36.7)
TRICARE and VA coverage	1.6 (0.0, 3.1)	2.9 (0.4, 5.3)	2.6 (0.6, 4.5)
Non-TRICARE civilian plan and VA coverage	1.9 (0.0, 3.7)	9.5 (5.0, 14.0)	7.7 (4.2, 11.1)
All three sources	2.4 (0.5, 4.3)	4.6 (1.5, 7.7)	4.1 (1.6, 6.5)
No prescriptions filled/paid for by any of these sources	0.5 (0.0, 1.6)	0.6 (0.0, 1.7)	0.6 (0.0, 1.5)

References

Atherly A., B. E. Dowd, and R. Feldman," The Effect of Benefits, Premiums, and Health Risk on Health Plan Choice in the Medicare Program," *Health Services Research,* Vol. 39, No. 4, 2004, pp. 847–864.

Buchmueller, T. C., and P. J. Feldstein, "The Effect of Price on Switching Among Health Plans," *Journal of Health Economics,* Vol. 16, 1997, pp. 231–247.

Bureau of Labor Statistics, *National Compensation Survey: Employee Benefits in Private Industry,* January 2005.

Congressional Budget Office, *Growth in Medical Spending by the Department of Defense,* September 2003. As of May 17, 2006:
http://www.cbo.gov/ftpdocs/45xx/doc4520/09-09-DoDMedical.pdf

Council of American Survey Research Organizations, "On the Definition of Response Rates," Port Jefferson, N.Y., 1982. As of January 30, 2007:
http://www.castro.org/resprates.cfm

Cutler, D. M., and S. J. Reber, "Paying for Health Insurance: the Trade-Off Between Competition and Adverse Selection," *Quarterly Journal of Economics,* 1998, pp. 433–466.

Defense Manpower Data Center, *2003 Survey of Retired Military: Administration, Datasets, and Codebook,* Arlington, Va., DC Report No. 2004 009, August 2004.

Goldman, D. P., A. A. Leibowitz, and D. A. Robalino, "Employee Responses to Health Insurance Premium Increases," *American Journal of Managed Care,* Vol. 10, 2004, pp. 41–47.

Hosek, Susan D., Bruce Bennett, Joan L. Buchanan, M. Susan Marquis, Kimberly A. McGuigan, Janet M. Hanley, Roger Madison, Afshin Rastegar, and Jennifer Hawes-Dawson, *The Demand for Military Health Care: Supporting Research for a Comprehensive Study of the Military Health Care System,* Santa Monica, Calif.: RAND Corporation, MR-407-1-OSD, 1995. As of February 5, 2007:
http://www.rand.org/pubs/monograph_reports/MR407-1/

Institute for Defense Analyses, *Evaluation of the TRICARE Program: Fiscal Year 2006 Report to Congress,* 2006. As of August 22, 2006:
http://www.tricare.osd.mil/planning/congress/downloads/FY2006_5.01.06.pdf

Kaiser Family Foundation and Health Research and Educational Trust, *Employer Health Benefits, 2004 Annual Survey,* Washington, D.C. 2004. As of May 17, 2006:
http://www.kff.org/insurance/7148/upload/2004-Employer-Health-Benefits-Survey-Full-Report.pdf

———, *Employer Health Benefits, 2005 Annual Survey,* Washington, D.C. 2005. As of August 17, 2006:
http://www.kff.org/insurance/7315/upload/7315.pdf

———, "Distribution of Out-of-Pocket Spending for Health Care Services," Web page, May 2006. As of January 30, 2007:
http://www.kff.org/insurance/snapshot/chcm050206.cfm

Office of the Assistant Secretary of Defense, Health Affairs, and the TRICARE Management Activity, "TRICARE Prime: Make an Appointment About MTFs," Web page, last updated October 11, 2006a. As of January 30, 2007:
http://www.tricare.mil/tricareprime/makeappt.cfm

————, "TRICARE Prime: Prime Compared to Standard," Web page, last updated October 11, 2006b. As of January 30, 2007:
http://www.tricare.mil/tricareprime/howprimecompares.cfm

————, "TRICARE Extra," Web page, last updated October 12, 2006c. As of January 30, 2007:
http://www.tricare.mil/tricareextra/default.cfm

————, "TRICARE Standard," Web page, last updated October 12, 2006d. As of January 30, 2007:
http://www.tricare.mil/tricarestandard/default.cfm

Ringel, Jeanne S., Susan D. Hosek, Ben A. Vollaard, and Sergej Mahnovski, *The Elasticity of Demand for Health Care: A Review of the Literature and Its Application to the Military Health System,* Santa Monica, Calif.: RAND Corporation, MR-1355-OSD, 2002. As of February 5, 2007:
http://www.rand.org/pubs/monograph_reports/MR1355/

Royalty, A. B., and N. Solomon, "Health Plan Choice: Price Elasticities in a Managed Competition Setting," *Journal of Human Resources,* Vol. 34, No. 1, 1999, pp. 1–41.

State Health Access Data Assistance Center and the Urban Institute, *Shifting Ground: Changes in Employer Sponsored Health Insurance,* report sponsored by the Robert Wood Johnson Foundation, 2006. As of May 17, 2006:
http://www.rwjf.org/newsroom/CTUWFinalResearchReport2006.pdf

Strombom, B. A., T. C. Buchmueller, and P. J. Feldstein, "Switching Costs, Price Sensitivity, and Health Plan Choice," *Journal of Health Economics,* Vol. 21, 2002, pp. 89–116.

U.S. Department of Labor, "FAQs About COBRA Continuation Health Coverage," undated Web page. As of January 30, 2007:
http://www.dol.gov/ebsa/faqs/faq_consumer_cobra.html